# Come, Holy Spirit

Fiftieth Anniversary Edition

# Come, Holy Spirit

*Thoughts on Renewing the Earth as the Kingdom of God*

Bishop Francis Xavier Ford, M.M.

With a New Introduction by Kevin J. Hanlon, M.M.

ORBIS BOOKS
Maryknoll, New York 10545

Founded in 1970, Orbis Books endeavors to publish works that enlighten the mind, nourish the spirit, and challenge the conscience. The publishing arm of the Maryknoll Fathers and Brothers, Orbis seeks to explore the global dimensions of the Christian faith and mission, to invite dialogue with diverse cultures and religious traditions, and to serve the cause of reconciliation and peace. The books published reflect the views of their authors and do not represent the official position of the Maryknoll Society. To learn more about Maryknoll and Orbis Books, please visit our website at www.orbisbooks.com.

---



Originally published in 1953 as *Come, Holy Ghost* by the Catholic Foreign Mission Society of America, Maryknoll, NY.

Published by Orbis Books, Box 302, Maryknoll, NY 10545-0302.



Manufactured in the United States of America.

---

Library of Congress Control Number: 2025947610

ISBN 978-1-62698-670-1 (print)

ISBN 979-8-88866-124-6 (ebook)

# Contents

# Introduction to the Fiftieth Anniversary Edition

**Kevin J. Hanlon, M.M.**

How happy I was to hear that there would be a printing of a Fiftieth Anniversary Edition of Bishop Ford's *Come, Holy Spirit*. As one Maryknoll priest trying to follow in his footsteps, I've grown to know our bishop more deeply over the past decade because of occasional requests to speak and write about him. He is now honored by the church as a *Servus Dei*, a "Servant of God." In my opinion, if anybody were to make a list of the top ten priests of the last century, the name Francis Xavier Ford would have to be on it (and near the top). Learning more about him enables any Catholic to know essential parts of the history of the church of the last century. His life and deeds also contain historical lessons on the interchange between Christianity and the nations it serves. Finally, the way he died is a testament to Christ's words, "No one has greater love than this, to lay down one's life for one's friends" (John 15:30).

The book is blessed to have an introduction written by the late Franciscan scholar Fr. Benedict Groeschel, who was a beloved professor at our former Maryknoll School of Theology. Catholics everywhere may remember Fr. Benedict's skill at explaining difficult Catholic teachings in print, on television, and in various other media. To illustrate the great mysteries, he used words the average "man and woman in the pew" could understand. But Groeschel's introduction to *Come, Holy Spirit* impresses us with the erudite way he explains both Christian and other mystical traditions, and shows Bishop Ford's spirituality in relation to these. This short introductory essay of Fr. Benedict's is, in a way, a mini-course on various world spiritual traditions through the lens of Bishop Ford's writings.

Fr. Groeschel also provides us with a good account of Bishop Ford's life, so I will not repeat the same here. However, I would like to add some insights into *Come, Holy Spirit* that I've garnered over the past years of researching Maryknoll's cofounders and her early notable missionaries.

In every age, the Lord says, "See, I am doing something new! . . . Do you not perceive it?" (Isaiah 43:19). For the young seminarian Francis Ford, this "something new" was the foundation of Maryknoll in 1911. He became its first candidate, for he had long felt a call to the mission field. In Maryknoll, the United States would now have its own missionary order of priests and brothers (soon followed by the sisters), and it would grow by leaps and bounds. The young seminarian from Brooklyn dared to leave his native land to venture into the unknown.

One might think, then, that he was the outgoing adventurous type, but he was known to be (and knew himself as) more of an introvert. As a seminarian, during free time, he would often take a book down to the woods behind the seminary and read. We are thankful that he had this tendency, because in *Come, Holy Spirit*, it is obvious that he is well read, quoting authors from various fields.

One of his first citations is from is from Pope Leo XIII, who wrote the first papal encyclical ever written on the Holy Spirit, *Divinus Illud Munus*, in 1897; this was written just five years after Ford was born. This encyclical letter started theological discussions on the Holy Spirit that would influence the Second Vatican Council in the 1960s. In his letter, Leo XIII recognized that Catholics were not always keeping the Holy Spirit front and center. He said we should remember St. Augustine's teaching that, just as the human soul has a body to dwell in, so the Holy Spirit is the soul of Christ's body, the church. Leo XIII also spoke of the Holy Spirit's "external mission," which began at Pentecost. His letter on the Holy Spirit must have been an inspiration for Bishop Ford, who chose to write on the Holy Spirit's role in "Renewing the Earth as the Kingdom of God" (the subtitle of his book).

After his ordination, Ford was sent with Maryknoll's first mission group to Canton (now Guangzhou) in 1918. After seven years as a missionary there, Father Ford was named the leader of the Apostolic Prefecture of Kaying (now called Meixian) in 1925, over two hundred miles away from Canton. He was only thirty-three years old. He certainly needed to rely on the Holy Spirit more than ever. He became head of an area that the Vatican hoped could become a diocese in the future, which it did. After leading the local church to much growth, the "Apostolic Prefect" Ford was made "Bishop Ford" in 1935 and served in that role until his death.

His coworkers in this mission were many other Maryknoll priests and brothers, but he had also invited the Maryknoll Sisters into his diocese. Instead of being limited only to institutions as most sisters on the missions were at the time (schools, orphanages, and the like), he asked them to also to preach the gospel directly. They would be trained and travel out two by two to remote villages to personally evangelize the women of the countryside. This groundbreaking mission methodology met with success. Some years ago, I met a sister who had worked with Bishop Ford when she was in her twenties, and she spoke of him with great warmth and appreciation. She felt that Bishop Ford had esteemed them and challenged them to be more. Although she must have been over ninety years of age when she talked to me, her spirit became very young when remembering her time in Kaying.

I mention all this because the book *Come, Holy Spirit* began its life as a series of talks that Bishop Ford first gave to the Maryknoll Sisters. The sisters' spiritual, theological, and pastoral needs were of direct concern to him. He understood that they were undergoing the same sort of trials that the men were, that of living in a faraway poor country, surrounded by vastly different language, history, and customs. He knew they would be tempted with discouragement and doubt. His solution was a more intimate spiritual life with the Holy Spirit. His presentations (the chapters in this book) have a balance of using both men and women figures to make his points. He talks of St. Thomas Aquinas and St. Ignatius of Loyola, but also cites the lives of St. Agnes, St. Teresa of Avila, and St. Catherine of Siena. He refers to G. K. Chesterton and Thornton Wilder, but also relies on words of Mother Mary Joseph Rogers (the foundress of the Maryknoll Sisters) and of Dorothy Day (who is also now named a "Servant of God" by the church). And not forgetting his roots, he also tells a story of his own mother, about her wisdom when dealing with the topic of love.

He knew that Maryknollers in China felt powerless over the suffering people endured from grim poverty and political upheavals, and proposed faith and prayer to the Holy Spirit to sustain them. And he also sees the Holy Spirit working through the people in China to sustain their missionaries: the fervor of these new Christians would increase the missionaries commitment to forging ahead. Their particular way of living the faith in trying circumstances was inspiring. The faith of the people strengthened the faith of their pastors. As missionaries are fond of saying these days, mission is a "two-way street," meaning that the missionary does not simply give a gift but also receives a gift from the people.

Bishop Ford wrote this work not knowing the way in which he would die. Like all good missionaries, he was hoping to be faithful to the end in spending his life for Christ his church. He probably thought, early on, that he would go like Fr. Thomas Frederick Price, his superior when they went to China, who died of illness only a year after their disembarking on Chinese soil. However, as China disintegrated into civil war, missionaries knew of the growing possibility of imprisonment and worse. Many were ordered home to wait for a time of peace. However, as the shepherd of his diocese, Bishop Ford stayed, hoping for the possibility of dialogue and compromise with the new government. Instead, he, as one of the few foreigners who had stayed in China, was scapegoated as a spy, arrested, abused on a long march to prison, neglected in his incarceration, and died there. Maryknoll Sister Joan Marie Ryan, an accomplished missionary in her own right, was Bishop Ford's secretary at the time of his arrest. She was also arrested and marched with him to prison, suffering many of the same hardships. During the long months in prison, she occasionally was able to catch glimpses of him in the yard, and saw him grow weaker and become emaciated, finally "looking like an old man of a hundred years."[1]

Bishop Ford's book on the Holy Spirit anticipated the work of the Second Vatican Council a decade later, a council that would emphasize more prominently the work and life of the Holy Spirit in the church: the Spirit is alive not only in her sacraments, but in the life and participation of the faithful in her mission. His book also indicates how he was able to endure such suffering until the end through his intimate union with Christ in the Holy Spirit. It was a spiritual union he wished for all those he pastored.

I thought of Bishop Ford recently when reading our late Holy Father's last homily for World Mission Sunday in 2024.[2] The pope compared the gospel passage of that Sunday, the Parable of the Wedding Banquet in the Gospel of Matthew, to the spreading of the gospel. Pope Francis says, "Mission, we see, is a tireless going out to all men and women, in order to invite them to encounter

---

[1] Sister Joan Marie Ryan, M.M., quoted in John F. Donavan, M.M., *The Pagoda and the Cross: The Life of Bishop Ford of Maryknoll* (NY: Scribner, 1967), 200.

[2] *Message of His Holiness Pope Francis for World Mission Sunday 2024: "Go and Invite Everyone to the Banquet" (Mt: 22:9)*, October 20, 2024. Available at www.vatican.va.

God and enter into communion with him. Tireless!" And he adds, "I take this opportunity to thank all those missionaries who, in response to Christ's call, have left everything behind to go far from their homeland and bring the Good News to places where people have not yet received it."

Bishop Ford left "everything behind" to serve people far away and grew to know even more about the Holy Spirit through his life on mission. I am grateful that he took the time to share what he learned by writing this book, because it can be a great help for any follower of Christ. It is my prayer that his words will inspire others, in their own particular vocations, to live and give their lives with the same dedication he did.

# Introduction

A glance through *Come, Holy Spirit* will reveal that it was written in a style and with a rhetoric that is no longer popular. The importance of the book at this time is not its style, but its content. It offers an insight into the soul of a man who was eventually to pay for his spiritual convictions with his life. In some ways it also gives an insight into the entire missionary effort of the American Catholic Church in the first part of the twentieth century. Bishop Ford in *Come, Holy Spirit* illuminates the motivations, aspirations, and convictions which led thousands of Americans to leave home and homeland to work as foreign missionaries. But the book does even more. It offers a penetrating look into the soul of a very remarkable human being, a man of immense determination and faith, a man who, I believe, shared in the ancient and profound experience of the Spirit called mysticism.

*Come, Holy Spirit* should be read and re-read carefully as a keyhole into a soul by anyone interested in an American form of spirituality. Contemporary interest in the spiritual and mystical more than justifies study of Bishop Ford's writings at this time.

The external facts of Francis Ford's life are startling only in their conclusion. He was born in Brooklyn in January of 1892 into a family which was totally dedicated to the establishment of the American Catholic Church. His father was the editor of Catholic journals whose overall thrust was the creation of a viable, intellectually respectable, politically independent and powerful Catholic community in Ireland and in the United States. The Catholicism of his youth was highly articulate, rationalistic rather than mystical, but withal inspired by a concern for others and a strain of the gentle affection for Christ, the Virgin Mother, and the Saints which was the legacy of medieval Irish spirituality. The attitudes of the time were an interesting counterpoint of the logic of St. Thomas Aquinas and the militancy of St. Ignatius Loyola on the one hand, and the affective mysticism of St. Francis of Assisi and St. Teresa of Avila on the other.

It was almost predictable that Francis Ford would become a priest of the Church, for it formed the whole sociocultural framework of his life. It was far less predictable that he would in 1912 join the very new Catholic Foreign Mission Society of America (Maryknoll). This missionary effort was just beginning in the immigrant American Church, but Frank Ford had got it into his head that his one ambition in life was to die the glorious death of a martyr. Some students of psychology might pounce on this detail of Ford's boyhood dreams and pronounce his life a self-fulfilling prophecy. However, a student of the psychology of mysticism might, on the other hand, see this dream as one of the most persistent signs of a life that is to be consumed by the awesome reality called the Divine Presence. The dream led to China and decades of devoted, energetic, and frequently dangerous work as a missionary priest and bishop. The stormy events of political history involve all sorts of people who are concerned with these struggles only in a secondary way. But since the interplay of political events affects the lives and needs of human beings so directly, any deeply spiritual person will be involved both intellectually and emotionally. Such an involvement, deeply personal and human, is seen in every chapter of *Come, Holy Spirit.*

Sometime between April 1951, when Bishop Ford was condemned by a "people's court" in China, and February 1952, he died. Sister Joan Marie, his secretary, was told at the end of her imprisonment that he had died of "old age." When one considers that the powerful have from time immemorial believed that it is expedient for holy and dedicated spiritual men and women to die for the people, the precise political reasons for Bishop Ford's death are of less importance. Anyone familiar with history will suspect that one day the children of those responsible for the death of this dedicated man will gratefully build his tomb. They may even pray to him for his tormentors.

Now let us look more deeply into this testament of Bishop Ford. *Come, Holy Spirit* falls roughly into two parts. The first is contemplative and the second more practical. Both parts reveal the soul of Francis Ford, although the second is more startling because it contains much of what is prophetic. Since it was not Bishop Ford's intention to write an autobiography, all of the revelations of his inner life are indirect. However, this makes the insights more meaningful and less studied. His words reveal the life and human experience of a man as he saw it. I will try to show that his words ring true when compared to the vision of the world that is held by the mystics. Mystics are those rare people found among all classes and kinds of human beings who have the ability to see a hidden reality beyond the world of superficial social convention which ordinarily organizes our lives. The word "mystic" originally comes from a Greek word meaning to "close one's eyes." It describes the person who has seen an inner vision unknown to the physical organs of perception. When accepted fully, this vision radically reorganizes one's set of values.

It was a surprise to many of my friends at Maryknoll when I told them I had discovered a mystic in their midst. Maryknoll breathes a purely American spirit—a spirit that is practical, energetic, and determined to get the apostolic job done efficiently. What did Maryknoll have to do with mystics, my friends asked. It is a tribute to the Maryknollers that my discovery of a mystic was a surprise but not an unpleasant one. Perhaps one can find the reason in the founders of Maryknoll. Archbishop

Walsh, Father Price, and Mother Mary Rogers once caused a bit of self-confessed astonishment to the young Frank Ford, who as a seminarian thought of them as a bit too contemplative (cf. Chapter 8). It is obvious in this little book that Frank Ford did not forget the lesson which as an energetic young seminarian he was not able to understand. It should be interesting to look for indications in this book of how he came to understand. The procedure will simply be to search for the cardinal principles of the spiritual life as described in the classics of spirituality, Christian and non-Christian, and see to what extent they are represented in Ford's thoughts.

*Come, Holy Spirit* opens with a line that puts Francis Ford as a mature man clearly in the line of Christian spiritual writers of the mystical tradition. "Our work will never save our souls. It is immaterial where we are or what we do; the thing that matters is who we are and what we intend." The primacy of intention is the basic operational insight of the spiritual life, the principle of action for anyone who ever wishes to pursue the mystic quest. These words of Bishop Ford place his thoughts in the broad spectrum of teachings reaching from the ancient Eastern religions to contemporary Christianity. They are reflections in modern thought forms of fundamental teachings of the Hindu scripture, the Bhagavad-Gita, "What you desire, that you become." This insight is consistent with Christian mystical writers from Ignatius of Antioch to Thomas Merton.

As the reader goes on, it will become apparent that the primacy of intention and desire, while they are the operational or pragmatic principles of Bishop Ford's life, do not provide the underlying theme of the meditations. The theme of his book, and I suspect of his life, is rather the awareness of the divine indwelling, presented in the familiar Catholic terms as the presence of the Holy Spirit in the soul. His words would be understood by the followers of any of the great religions of the world. "If instead of saying, 'in the state of grace,' we spoke of God dwelling in us, we might see this wonderful truth in a clearer light. We share in the divine life, we become participators in the divine life, sharers in the Blessed Trinity." This insight, expressed in terms both universal and yet orthodoxly Catholic, is the unifying theme of the whole series of meditations. Bishop Ford reveals that it is the motivating force of his life. Anyone who survives seminary training or theological studies knows that the insight of the divine indwelling remains a sterile theological conceptualization unless it transfigures the world that the person perceives, unless spontaneously and without effort it colors the whole of one's life. Dean William Inge, an Anglican scholar, in his classic work, *Christian Mysticism* (Meridian Books) writes, "Mysticism may be defined as the attempt to realize in thought and feeling the immanence of the temporal in the eternal and the eternal in the temporal." Throughout *Come, Holy Spirit* this immanence is clearly seen. But the reader may be tempted to feel that I am using the words of Bishop Ford, which after all are to be found in any typical handbook of theology, in a contrived way to make him seem like a mystic.

One has only to understand Inge's explanation of mysticism and then to look at Ford's life and words to see that this is not the case. Inge affirms the necessary role mysticism plays in providing not only the initial insight of religion but also in reviving the vitality of this insight when the experience has ceased. Otherwise, the symbols that embody these insights either petrify or evaporate, two distinct processes which are fatal to religion. According to Inge, it is the historical function of mysticism, as an active independent principle, to revive the spirituality of religion in the midst of formalism and unbelief. True mysticism or, to use a less awesome word, spirituality, in all cases, and certainly in the case of Bishop Ford, is the spirit of revival and renewal. While anyone would admit that the life of a courageous martyr witnesses to the profundity of his faith, does this book bear out the further contention that Francis Ford was possessed of the inner vision or awareness of God which Inge speaks of?

Throughout the book are evidences of real insight into the immanence or presence of God in his own soul and in the world. He uses familiar mystical analogies, such as the "inner temple," friendship with God by the inpouring of divine love, and the totality of the divine Presence. It is characteristic of mystics that the immanence or possession of God in their souls projects into the world about them, so that the universe becomes sacramentalized. This is the quality of mystics which makes them most appealing to others. This awareness of the immanence of God is spontaneous and absorbing. We are familiar with this insight in the Gospels, in Hammarskjold and Teilhard in our own time, and in a great many mystics in between. It is particularly clear in the life of St. Francis. Bishop Ford, this apparently practical apostle, was greatly impressed with the mystical quality of St. Francis. The tone of the following passage reveals more than a devout interest in the Poverello. It suggests a shared experience: "If we were utterly absorbed in the thought of the Holy Spirit, the giver of all good gifts, we would know the ecstasy experienced by St. Francis of Assisi. . . . He called the sun his brother and the moon his sister. Fire and water were to St. Francis pure and radiant symbols of the Holy Spirit." "St. Francis used to rejoice in seeing the Holy Spirit but for us it is more difficult." If one reads *Come, Holy Spirit* with this luminous quality in mind, the pages will come alive. Perhaps Dean Inge's view that formalism and the weakness of faith require mysticism to revive our religion might point out why we find the direct use of the symbols of faith by Bishop Ford tedious. Some people only see flowers when they walk through a meadow and others see the lilies of the field.

Before moving on to the more practical level of the book, the moral portion as it were, something must be said about Bishop Ford's very explicit and precise use of the formulas of faith in what our age might consider a naive application of these formulas. Speaking of religious obedience, Bishop Ford might make many, save the most preconciliar Catholics, squirm a bit. "Throughout the Christian centuries Catholics have given obedience to the Pope, the Vicar of Christ on earth. This obedience has made the Catholic Church the most powerful religious unit in the world." In these days, one as devoted to the Holy See as I am myself might find a different mode of expression of my loyalty and of basically the same convictions. The question is, does such a specifically conceptualized Catholicism square with mysticism and the universal visions of spirituality?

In the popular conception of mystics they are often pictured as synthetic and comprehensive, if not a bit vague and ethereal. Because their experience of God has been highly individualistic they are often portrayed as religious rebels. They have often been in trouble because of their seeming hyperbole and a tendency to see all things more related to each other than do the rest of their coreligionists. This view of mysticism is in fact a misconception. All the great mystics of the world, despite their individual experiences of God, have oddly enough remained drawn to an orthodox adherence to the faith which divine providence had them born into or led to as adults. None of them ever came to destroy the law and the prophets. Mystics, unlike many other religious personalities, are "yes" sayers, and not "no" sayers. Evelyn Underhill, the great scholar of mysticism, writing in the early part of the twentieth century, describes this apparent paradox in her work on the spiritual life, *The Essentials of Mysticism*. "This common opinion that the mystic is a lonely soul wholely absorbed in his vertical relationship with God, that his form of religious life represents an opposition to and an implicit criticism of the corporate and institutional forms of religious life, this is decisively contradicted by history which shows us again and again the great mystics as loyal children of the great religious institutions, and forces us to admit that here as in other departments of human activity the corporate and individual life are intimately plaited together." This unusual insight alone solves the riddle of the "mystical missionary" presented by the life of Francis Ford. The orthodoxy of the mystic goes beyond an allegiance to a creed based partly on social or even personal identity. At that elementary level a person may be shaken into belief or unbelief by his own self concept and by how he sees himself fitting into the world around him. The common run of the mill believer is vulnerable to religious inconsistency in behavior or, what may be more dangerous, reacting to a popular rejection of what he had come to accept as the word of God. The most tragic example of this is the apostles' failure of faith at Gethsemane. Their immature faith crumbled despite their very personal human experience with the Lord because their contemporaries directly challenged the credibility of the Master. The only one of them to remain loyal was the young man who would one day write that believers were born not of the will of the flesh, nor of the will of men, but were the children of God.

The faith born of God is a special sign of the mystic. It is what St. Augustine alludes to when he writes that "no creature however rational or intellectual is enlightened of himself, but is enlightened by the participation in Eternal Truth." The universal teaching of mystics is that faith will be expressed in an orthodoxy which has little to do with social or personal reinforcement, but it is the profound intuition of the person touched by God. As the Hindu mystic, Ramakrishna, points out, "A man can only reach God if he follows one path rightly." The very explicit and precise formulation of faith used by Bishop Ford may, as it were, turn off some who would like to come to understand him. Perhaps the problem is theirs and not his. No person with spiritual depth will stay with words but will be led beyond and above them. To reject the words of traditional faith is not to go beyond them but to stumble beneath them. To see the Church of Christ simply as a sociological phenomena is to misunderstand Bishop Ford and every Catholic mystic. It is to fail to grasp Inge's formulation of spirituality as a vital force in faith. A mere sociological or historical view of the Church makes the death of martyrs a very questionable business indeed.

The conviction of Bishop Ford and his firm, vital, and orthodox adherence to the Catholic faith are perhaps best explained by another bishop and martyr, St. Ignatius of Antioch, who on his way to death advised the Christian community to maintain the sacramental character of faith. "Respect the bishop as the symbol of God, and the presbyters as the council of God, and the college of the apostles. Apart from them there is not even the name of a church." We are often accustomed to take professions of faith as formulas and perhaps even make them in a formalistic way ourselves. With the admonition of this ancient Father of the Church in mind and in the light of the mystical view of the Church as the sacramental sign of Christ, the Teacher, in the world, one ought to ponder these words of Bishop Ford: "We cannot imitate Our Lord Spirit to enable us to hear in the Church's laws the voice of Christ speaking to us. . . . As members of this living Body we breathe the Spirit of Christ when we obey its law." These words cannot be heard in any formalistic way when we know that the writer would someday shed his blood along the roads of that land to which the Church had sent him.

The later chapters of *Come, Holy Spirit* are largely moralistic—even at times "preachy" in a forgivable way. Telling people what to do and how to behave has been a pardonable fault of both martyrs and bishops from time immemorial. It is the tone of these moral lessons, rather than their predictable content, which is of interest in coming to know Francis Ford. This tone may be described as actively penitential in a very personalized way, enthusiastic, and yet filled with an awareness of imperfection.

From the beginning of the book you know that Bishop Ford is preaching to himself as a penitent: "We run to see what the Church teaches and then we make no further attempt to make these teachings our own by deep thoughts." If you have any doubts about whether these words are directed to himself, read on a few lines. "We have wasted our inheritance, the amazing inheritance described in the prayer said by the priest when putting on his cassock, 'The Lord is the portion of my inheritance.'" Indications that Francis Ford saw himself as a penitent are found throughout his whole meditations. But these are always set in a frame of enthusiasm for the present and the future. "We insult God afresh when we are discouraged by sin because we thereby confess that we do not have hope in the Passion of Our Savior and in the purifying power of God the Holy Spirit." This theme of God as the living Savior of the person burdened by sin is not popular in contemporary religious writing, but it is the characteristic moral attitude of mystical writers. In my opinion it is the moral aspect of the awareness of the divine indwelling; it is the response. The first letter of St. John sums up the Christian expression of this universally recognized mystical theme, "If we claim to be sinless, we are self-deceived and strangers to the truth. If we confess our sins, he is just, and may be trusted to forgive our sins and cleanse us from every kind of wrong" (John 1:8). The active awareness of personal sin and imperfection is something that does not fit well into the neuroses of our time. People interested in religion at present, and in a number of previous ages, have had a great need to feel already perfect—to believe that whatever they are doing is the best. A person of such a mind will find cold comfort in *Come, Holy Spirit*—and probably will be so annoyed that he may miss the dynamism of this opposite view. Bishop Ford's perception of himself as a very imperfect man, constantly struggling and yet constantly meeting the love of God, is in a way too energetic for an age that suffers from the depression characteristic of any identity crisis. Words like the following are a bit disconcerting: "God has filled our souls with a light so brilliant and powerful that sometimes we cannot even see it. . . . It would be well for us, then, to stand for a few moments in front of this light, fully conscious of its divine radiance." This description of enlightenment comes immediately after the confession of sin. It reminds me of the song of praise uttered by St. Augustine at the time of his conversion. Speaking of his release from vice, Augustine prayed, "How sweet all at once it was for me to be rid of those fruitless joys. . . . You drove them from me, you who are the true and sovereign joy, you who outshine all light and yet are hidden deeper than any secret in our hearts, you who surpass all honor though not in the eyes of men who see all honor in themselves" *(Confessions* IX, 1).

If one reads *Come, Holy Spirit* in the light of this unique attitude of the mystics—call it joyful enthusiastic penance—then the preaching does not sound like moralizing but rather creative affection for God and others.

The final question, so obvious that I have waited until the end of this exploration to introduce it, is how to fit the active life of a missionary into the mold of the mystic. Realistically, are not the two exclusive? Apparently early in Maryknoll's history this thinking was recognized as a false dichotomy. Mother Mary Joseph, foundress of the Maryknoll Sisters, hoped that they would be "working contemplatives." A specifically American idea? Perhaps, in its mode of presentation but not in its expression. Evelyn Underhill sums up the question well in the *Essentials of Mysticism*. "Taken as a class, the Christian mystics are distinguished by nothing so much as by their heroic and unselfish activities, by their varied and innumerable services to the corporate life of the Church. From their ranks have come missionaries, preachers, prophets, social reformers, poets, founders of institutions, servants of the poor and the sick, patient guides and instructors of souls."

That Bishop Ford saw loving service of his fellow man as the logical outcome of his prayer is too obvious to discuss. But he humbly admits that this work became something of a sublimation of self seeking and that

Father Price had corrected him. Then he describes how he learned from failure and hardship to purify his motives. He writes several times that he found strength to go on in spite of frustration, and he illustrates his point by citing the difficulties of St. Teresa and St. John of the Cross, two splendid mystics of the Church. Like them, his strength he finds in the Cross, and in the grace of Christ. Before we dismiss this as a pious platitude, compare his words with the observation of Underhill: "If his [the mystic's] special claim to communion with the transcendent be true at all, then he does really tap a source of vitality higher than that with which other men have contact. . . . This larger and intenser vitality the mystic does not and cannot keep to himself." And so the forces of the life of Francis Ford were moving very clearly—dedication, labor, and love, heroic and founded in God. His enemies were ultimately only *dramatis personae*. His preoccupation with them as foes when he sought to convert them by prayer (if by no other means) is really only incidental. They would be ultimately only as important as Herod, or Pilate, or Longinus, the Centurion, who eventually was converted. One can see the vision of the martyr coming into focus as the book ends with the startling prophecy: "It may be that in the years to come, some of us will be called upon to suffer persecution at the hands of Communists. . . . Persecution was given us as a legacy and a promise by our Savior, and as a mark of identification with him. . . . Let us offer ourselves, then, to be consumed as a holocaust, burned up in the flaming charity of God the Holy Spirit, the Spirit of Love."

The last friend to see him alive, Sister Joan Marie, his secretary, caught sight of him after he had been dragged along the roads by his captors. How one is struck by these words; "It needs more training to seek God among the rough stones of the dusty road than in the beauty of the sunset."

Much more could be written about Francis Ford—and we may hope it will be written. Much must wait to be written until time has healed the wounds of the world. I believe that he will have a message for a later time which may be able to evaluate him better. For us in our own time of transition, of identities lost and found, I think that his message is one of the importance of spiritual freedom. This may seem paradoxical. He was so involved, so committed, at times apparently so compelled by inner forces, how can one call him free? The answer is that very strong identity, which made him free to face all sorts of forces that intimidate most human beings—failure, doubt, human cupidity, fear, even death. But one only understands this identity and freedom of action when one understands the mystical insight from which it sprang. The relationship between the mystical vision of the Holy Spirit and freedom was explored by Edward I. Watkin in the *Philosophy of Mysticism* (Harcourt, Brace) in words that can be an effective guide in reading *Come, Holy Spirit:* "The soul must submit its will in all things to the will of God. Thus alone can it be free from all limitations. . . . In proportion as the soul effects this submission . . . it becomes freer to follow the voice of conscience illuminated by grace and later by mystical intuition, a voice which tells her plainly that the infinite and the absolute Divine Goodness is the only true end of her actions and life. . . . Wholly to submit, to be one with the will of God is to become perfectly free because it is the destruction of all limits. . . . This is the freedom of the sons of God, led by the Holy Spirit of God who is the eternal love of Absolute Goodness for Absolute Goodness." *Come, Holy Spirit* indicates that Francis Ford, when he wrote this book, was moving toward being such a free man.

Fr. Benedict Joseph Groeschel, O.F.M. Cap.
Trinity Retreat
Larchmont, New York

# One

# Come, Holy Spirit

Our work will never save our souls. It is immaterial where we are and what we do; the thing that matters is who we are and what we intend. Constant preoccupation with exterior work handicaps our knowledge of ourselves and of our intentions. Of course, God takes that handicap into consideration, but we cannot afford to do so. We know that we often go through whole days, perhaps whole weeks, of being lost in our work without stopping to take a breath.

After the first hundred yards, the runner in a race begins to find breathing painful, then he slows down to regulate his breath. He doesn't stop breathing, but somehow or other he controls his breathing apparatus and gets what we call second wind. Once he gets this second wind, he can go on running until his legs give out.

In his spiritual progress, the Christian has the same need of regulating and renewing his inner life. These breathing spaces should not be for him, any more than for the runner, times of relaxation. During his long working days, he has tried to cooperate physically and mentally with God; now he must give interior cooperation, a more strenuous effort. But he need not rely solely on his own strivings to gain that second wind. "Come, Holy Spirit, Thou in labor rest most sweet."

Many of us find it difficult to think about the Holy Spirit. As Pope Leo XIII said in his great Encyclical on the Holy Spirit, our faith in the Third Person of the Blessed Trinity "is involved in much darkness." Yet we could not think about a more absorbing subject. I, personally, as a bishop, have a special obligation to know and to preach the Holy Spirit. In my consecration I received the plenitude of priestly power, so I literally give the Holy Spirit at ordination and through the ministry of my priests.

## Sharers in the Blessed Trinity

St. Paul says that the Holy Spirit is "the Spirit of adoption of sons, whereby we cry: Abba, Father" *(Rom. VIII: 15).* We receive God the Holy Spirit from the first instant of our baptism and He is truly present within us from then on, unless we willfully dislodge Him from our souls by mortal sin. We become temples of the Holy Spirit. He doesn't merely dwell with us externally; He becomes one with us.

We call the Holy Spirit the Sanctifier. He makes us holy; indeed, He does more than that. Through Him we become godlike, partakers of the nature of God. We become one with God through the action of the Holy Spirit. From the instant of our baptism, God takes possession of us. We share in the divine life. As regards quality, we share as fully as the saints in heaven; but we do not share to the same degree, and soul differs from soul in the sharing.

We say that when we have sanctifying grace, we are in the state of grace and we are using words that mean very little to us. If instead of saying, in the state of grace, we spoke of God dwelling in us, we might see this wonderful truth in a clearer light. We share in the divine life, we become participators in the divine life, sharers in the Blessed Trinity. There is nothing more startling than this amazing evidence of God's Love for us, nothing more worthy of our study.

The Church is accustomed to attribute to God the Father those works of the Divinity in which power excels; to God the Son those in which wisdom excels; and those in which love excels to God the Holy Spirit. The Holy Spirit proceeds externally as the mutual love of the Father and the Son. So, because the indwelling of God in us is a union of love, it is attributed to God the Holy Spirit. Of course, all three Persons of the Blessed Trinity dwell in the soul of a baptized Christian in the state of grace. The Blessed Trinity never acts separately outside of Itself; and all actions are from God the Father, God the Son, and God the Holy Spirit.

When we receive our Lord in Holy Communion, He stays with us as long as the physical elements remain, which is a very short time; some say fifteen minutes, some say five. But the Spirit of Love, God the Holy Spirit, remains with us just as He remained in the heart of Our Lord when He dwelt on earth. We cannot see Him, any more than the contemporaries of Jesus could see the indwelling of the Holy Spirit in Christ.

## The Motive Power

We have been created to the divine life by God's love; and those of us who are apostles are dedicated to showing to souls in the shadow of death that God is Love. God's love for mankind is a possessing love, a yearning love, more so than any friendship on earth; and we have dedicated our lives to carrying the message of the Tremendous Lover to the whole world. "Send forth Thy Spirit and they shall be created." But what if we ourselves forget the message, even as we carry it, and so are not created to a new life? We shall have missed our vocation.

St. Catherine of Siena said that she made her heart a temple of God and she adored God in her heart. In our apostolic life we have to overcome the obstacles of discouragement, sin, tepidity, and lack of aim. We shall succeed only if we find a motive behind our vocation. We are driven by Love, by God's Love. He is the motive power. So, the more clearly we realize our dependence on Him, the more surely we shall reach our goal. He is coming to us Who will teach us all things. He will compensate for the absence of Himself in pagan surroundings. He is the light that we are to bring to others in darkness. So, we must become actively conscious of His presence, of His power, of His special love for us. It is His will that we carry out in our work; and we must know that will.

Do we understand our dependence on the Holy Spirit for the purifying of our daily lives? If we are testing a piece of cloth, we hold it up to the light to see the imperfections in it. In like manner, we should undertake to hold up our souls before the light of the Holy Spirit. Our spiritual garments become soiled, and they need mending. We have to examine them as the searchlight of the Holy Spirit shines through them.

It is a waste of time to expend our energy fruitlessly, if there is no motive behind it. If we shut out God the Holy Spirit from our daily work, it becomes vitiated by pride, jealousy, and all the vices that are running rampant in the world today and causing enmity among the nations. G.K. Chesterton pointed out that before the coming of Christ, the pagans practiced many virtues.

There were Vestal Virgins before there were Catholic virgins; and the Stoic manifested heroic fortitude. But one virtue was lacking among the ancient pagans: the Christian virtue of humility, the recognition of their own weaknesses. The lack of this same Christian virtue of humility among modern pagans is back of all the crime in the world.

## Love Bridges the Chasm

The infallible Church teaches us to pray, "Come, Holy Spirit." Without any formalities, we order the Third Person of the Blessed Trinity to inundate our human hearts with divine love! Earthly potentates, and even minor officials, would be offended if we presumed to address them in this manner. If we send a letter to a Chinese notable and do not employ the proper honorific terms in addressing him, he does not acknowledge our communication.

Only Divine Charity is never puffed up. God's Love bridges the chasm between our littleness and His Omnipotence; and it pleases the Holy Spirit to hear us trustfully ordering Him to come with the fullness of Love into our hearts.

## Two

# Come, Thou Father of the Poor

We might say that a Christian has not fulfilled the purpose of his life unless he becomes conscious of the presence of God in his soul, in the very depth of his being, in a union that is closer than any other on earth. In the Hymn for Pentecost, one of the few hymns the Church has adopted, we find the words: "Come, Holy Spirit, send forth the radium of Thy heavenly light." That hymn was written in England in the thirteenth century by Archbishop Stephen Langton, and it is curious that he should have used the word "radium," which describes so wonderfully the action of the Holy Spirit on the Christian soul.

Radium can penetrate even through the walls of a building and affect objects at a distance. In X-ray therapy, it penetrates tissues that are deformed. In like manner, God the Holy Spirit is the radium of the Christian soul.

We must see life in the verity of His heavenly light, through the penetrating, curing warmth of His love.

## In the Light of God's Radium

Stephen Langton goes on to say: "Come, Thou Father of the poor." We are the richest of God's creatures, we have everything, the whole world is given to us. Chesterton points out that one of the greatest dangers for Catholics is spiritual pride, because we have everything necessary for happiness and spiritual health. How, then, can we think of God the Holy Spirit as the "Father of the poor?" It will not be difficult to do so if we realize that our splendid Christian inheritance is given to us gratis, a gift that we have not earned and which we cannot rightfully call our own. It is God's. All that we have done is to impoverish ourselves.

We are truly poor. We have misused the little we do possess of our own: our will, our understanding, our heart throbs, our motives. We have often withheld our cooperation with God the Holy Spirit, and the little we have given has been distorted and grudgingly yielded. The light of God's radium brings out in stark clarity the poverty of our souls, not to make us pessimistic or hopeless, but to destroy cancerous self-deception and hypocrisy.

Spiritual pride can take on very odd kinks. We pride ourselves, unconsciously at least, on our apostolic successes. We distort the truth to ourselves in regard to our motives. We usually discover our motive after the accomplishment of an action. Then, when we are telling others what we have done, we attribute to ourselves a high spiritual motive. The truth is that our good actions are often prompted by mere inclination. We are doing what we like to do.

The conversation of priests and religious is much taken up with religious subjects and with their daily work. They are used to the "clap-trap" phrases concerning spiritual motives; and they unconsciously add them on to the story of their doings, in order to embellish the tale a little bit. They are not doing it maliciously, but it is possible in this way to develop a nice little case of hypocrisy.

Even to ourselves, we pretend reasons and motives that are in reality afterthoughts. It is so easy to find excuses for our failures; there is always some extenuating circumstance that was not our fault. A very good proof that we were at fault is the fact that we are elaborating these extenuating circumstances. We are acting in self-defense.

We would not need to justify ourselves so painstakingly, if we were not endeavoring to salve an uneasy conscience. We feel called upon to explain exactly why it was not our mistake that caused the failure, but not to admit simply that there was something wrong in our motive. In this we are poor; and we need to test our sincerity with ourselves and with God, in the light of God's radium that penetrates all the tortuous little secret places of the human soul.

## Wasted Inheritance

We are poor in thoughts about God. Apostles are supposed to be the masters from whom others derive their knowledge of God; and yet, how halfhearted we are in our own efforts to grow in the knowledge of God. We hastily refresh our memories of essentials for a given occasion; we learn by heart, and we are not above passing off the material memorized as our own thoughts. We have so few deeply apprehended thoughts of our own.

In her book, *Union Square to Rome,* Dorothy Day speaks of the sincere efforts of Communists to study their beliefs. They meet together in restaurants, or dance halls, or wherever they have arranged for their social gathering, and exchange thoughts on Communist teachings. Of course, some of these conversations are superficial; but many of them are sincere and deep and well thought out.

Chesterton, also, emphasizes how wholehearted the Communists are in their efforts to apprehend thoroughly their system. They consecrate all their powers to one purpose. If they manifest such an intense desire to think things out clearly, in order to teach men how to achieve temporal well-being on this earth, should we lag so far behind in zeal in preparing to teach the ineffable joys of the Kingdom of God? Come, Holy Spirit, and fructify our poor, parched thoughts.

The Protestant reformers wished to rely entirely on individual interpretation of the lights received from the Holy Spirit. In our reaction against the Reformation, we have so emphasized authority and whatever the Church teaches that we have a tendency to take a passive view on all matters. We run to see what the Church teaches, and then make no further attempt to make the teaching our own by deep thoughts. We take the remedy before we get the disease; we take the corrective before we have gone wrong.

God intended us to use the lights of the Holy Spirit and then, for fear of going wrong, to compare them with the teachings of the Church. We use the inspirations of the Holy Spirit, and we channel them into the sure boundaries of the infallible Church; then we begin to see ourselves in the light of eternity. We realize how poor we are in our motives, in our thoughts, and in our actions.

Religious seek perfection by taking the vow of poverty. Our Lord said, "Blessed are the poor in Spirit." But I am not speaking now about either of these states of poverty pleasing to God. I am talking about the poor *of* spirit. We have wasted our inheritance, the amazing inheritance described in the prayer said by the priest when putting on his cassock: "The Lord is the portion of my inheritance."

## We Need Sincerity

In the evening, I help the Chinese students in our hostel with their English lessons. One of the stories they have in their readers is about a king who ordered a splendid robe for his coronation ceremony. But his spinners did not have any cloth, and they were afraid to say so. Instead, they began to spread the news that they were making a wonderful garment visible only to the wise and the sincere. The king sent his ministers to see the cloth while it was in the making.

The ministers saw the spinners busily making the motions of weaving, but no cloth was there. They were unwilling to admit that they were not wise, so they all admired the non-existent cloth. Finally, the poor king came and he couldn't see any cloth either; but he was just as much a hypocrite as the rest of them. He wore the imaginary garment for the coronation ceremony; and only a little child said very simply: "The king has nothing on."

That is the way we are. We parade about in supposed capabilities and supposed motives, taking the excellence of our spiritual garments for granted. It is marvelous how we preen ourselves and strut around as though we were persons of real consequence. Out of this are begotten all our jealousies, envy, and determination to maintain our own opinions no matter what others think. Then, the Father of the poor gives us another chance to see ourselves in all our spiritual destitution, in the radium of the Holy Spirit.

How sorely we need to listen to the inspirations of the Spirit of Truth. There is a terrible passage in Isaiah: "I called and you did not answer, I spoke and you did not hear. And you did evil in my eyes: and you have chosen the things that displease me. Therefore thus said the Lord God: Behold my servants shall eat, and you shall be hungry. . . . They shall rejoice, and you shall be confounded" *(Isai. LXV: 12–14).*

## God Calls the Prodigal

The Holy Spirit has given us all the means necessary to attain full union with Him and to be perfect in our work; but we are heedless in our prodigal waste of the inspirations received. St. Ignatius suggests that we note down these lights as we receive them, because we have odd minds. We can step out of the chapel and forget at once any thought that came to us while we were praying. This may be partly due to the generosity of heart with which we are immediately absorbed in whatever apostolic work we are doing; but St. Paul has warned us that they who preach to others may themselves become castaways.

As we see in black and white some trivial little resolution that we are proposing for ourselves, it comes as a shock to realize that we have fallen so far short of our ideal. This realization is not a reason for discouragement. If we place the lead of distrust between ourselves and God the Holy Spirit, the healing radium of His light cannot penetrate our souls. The Father of the poor asks only that, like the prodigal son in the Gospel, we "return to ourselves." Then His vivifying love floods and fructifies our barren hearts.

Talk of material poverty and poverty in spirit becomes hypocrisy, unless we are conscious that we have a poverty *of* spirit. We have to be sincere with ourselves and with God, realizing that we have abused and wasted our inheritance. We are prodigals who did not heed the loving suggestions of the Spirit of Truth. Now God has spoken to our conscience. Returning to ourselves, let us arise and go to the loving embrace of the Father of the poor.

## Three

# Come, Giver of All Gifts

We have seen that, because of ourselves we are nothing, we cannot advance in sanctity without the help of God the Holy Spirit, the Father of the poor. Now, let us look at the other side of the picture, for the Third Person of the Blessed Trinity is likewise the Giver of all gifts. In ourselves we are destitute; but through God we have everything. If we really understood how rich God's love makes us, we would never again be sad or discouraged.

If we were utterly absorbed in the thought of the Holy Spirit as the Giver of all good gifts, we would know the ecstasy experienced by St. Francis of Assisi. Some of the other friars used to dislike walking on the road with him, because they said that he was liable to make a fool of himself. Francis could not contain the expression of his joy, for he saw everything as a symbol of God, a gift of God. He called the sun his brother and the moon his sister. Fire and water were to Francis pure and radiant symbols of the Holy Spirit. He saw even the wolf of Gubbio as a gift of God, so that the ardor of the saint's charity made the fierce animal as gentle as a lamb.

Why should we find it so difficult to recognize God in His gifts to us? Have we not treasured during our lives many keepsakes that remind us of their givers? As we look at them, we see again clearly the faces of loved ones. So in the works of the Creator the saints become conscious with new joy of the Presence of God.

If our Chinese Christians were to come and place a present in front of us and we paid no attention to it, we would feel guilty. Yet that is what God is constantly doing to us. He is giving us presents all the time, and we pass them by. Christian life is not meant to be sad, and if we could see its daily events as gifts of a loving God, it would be supremely happy.

## Tokens of Love

Come, Holy Spirit, Giver of all good gifts. A gift is something deliberately presented to us personally as a token of love. So that everything we see around us should be labeled as gifts from the Holy Spirit with love. It is sometimes difficult to recognize the noise and bustle of a great city as coming from the Holy Spirit; but here in China we are blessed in being so close to nature. All the simple, beautiful things around us are special gifts to remind us of God's love.

This may all seem very elementary and childlike, but it is the language which Our Lord spoke while He was on earth. All His talks to the people were parables, about the flowers of the field and simple things. Even when Christ was about to give mankind the Gift of His Body and Blood in the Holy Eucharist, He acted without any pomp. He ate and drank with His Apostles, taking first a piece of bread and then a cup of wine they were drinking, and saying, "This is I. Take this Sacrament of Love as a Gift from Me, and remember Me when you receive It."

"Remember Me." God wants us to remember Him, not only in the reception of the Holy Eucharist, but in perceiving everything in the sacramental universe about us as tokens of His care for us. This is not merely a pious platitude. God has a message for us in every object that we encounter. If one of God's gifts does not remind us of the Divine Giver, then He seeks to attract us to Himself with another. The Holy Spirit is always trying to reach us by His gifts.

St. Francis of Assisi used to rejoice in seeing the Holy Spirit in the sacramental universe; but for us it is more difficult. In speaking of God the Father and God the Son we are using human terms that convey definite meaning to our minds; but when we speak of God the Holy Spirit, our human minds begin to falter and we have to fall back on symbols.

In the Scriptures, the Holy Spirit gave us symbols to aid our finite minds. He came in tongues of fire, in a rushing wind, and in the form of a dove. So we can think about Him as the Giver of light, of cleansing inspiration, and of peace. The wonder of these gifts can lift our hearts from their splendor to the Divine Charity of their Giver.

## Time Is a Gift

We can use God's gifts to His glory in thanking Him, or we can abuse these gifts by misunderstanding them. If we analyze our lives, we can see that all our hardships come from misunderstanding God's gifts. God's gift of time to us is one that we cannot afford to abuse or misunderstand. We must use time to achieve eternal happiness, to become saints.

One instant of time is enough in which to become a saint, and we have twenty-four hours a day all the days of our lives. But we don't know how many days still remain to us, so we have to recall constantly that what makes a saint is the right use of God's gift of time. Sins of omission can be a greater obstacle in some lives than sins of commission. We must be generous in turning back the gift of time in thanks to God, in using it for Him.

The warmth of our gratitude to God for the gift of time should urge us on to achieve holiness without delay. St. Agnes was only twelve or thirteen years old when she won the crown of martyrdom; but the strength of her union with the Holy Spirit was so great that she withstood all the powers of Imperial Rome.

## Buried Talents

It seems to me that the greatest misuse we make of God's gifts to us is the misuse of our talents. There is a false sort of humility that makes us say, "I cannot do that; I am not fitted for that work." We sometimes hold back, and do not expend all our abilities on the task at hand.

On analysis, we discover that the work we hold back on is a task assigned to us by others, and not some pet project of our own. If we propose a plan of work and it is given to us to carry out, we go into it with heart and soul. Then someone else suggests a modification of our plan, and our ardor slackens. We discover reasons why we cannot cope with the task any longer. This is not humility, but the pettiness of wounded pride.

In the apostolic life, we don't talk about our abilities, because we would consider that as a sign of pride. But we think just the same that we have good abilities, and we flatter ourselves on being resigned to humble tasks. All that this means is that we are resigned to holding back, to a neglect of the talents God has given us. We will not be given any duty that is beyond our abilities, because all that we are asked to do is the best we can. So, why not at all times pour out all our talents in the service of God? Yet, how often we are niggardly and slovenly in the use of the gifts God has bestowed on us. In our teaching of Catechism, we are too often content with routine efforts. If a person does not appeal to us, we do not use all our talents to win him by charity. If we have set our heart on some task, and are assigned instead one that we consider inferior, it is amazing how incompetent we suddenly become. Yet we all know, in theory at least, that in the service of God it is not the task that matters but our intention and how we do it. From childhood we have been familiar with the parable of the man who buried his talents, instead of putting them to good use in his master's service; but somehow it does not come home to us that we, too, are unprofitable servants.

## Divine Invitations

How often and how glibly we speak about examination of conscience. By reason of its very familiarity, the expression loses much of its force. We might be roused to greater spiritual effort by a challenge to examine our fidelity to the lights granted us by the Holy Spirit, and by asking ourselves how consistently we have accepted the divine invitations contained in His gifts.

"To those who love God, all things work together unto good, to those who are called to be saints" *(Rom. VIII: 28).*

Come, Thou Giver of all gifts and create in us by the fire of love a new heart, so that Thy invitations may be visible to us alike in the slime of our earthly pilgrimage and in the glory of the firmament studded with stars.

## Four

# Come, Light of the Soul

Apostles have a special need of the indwelling of God the Holy Spirit to be a light to their hearts. This is true whether their work is among people ignorant of the Faith, or among modern pagans who have exchanged their Christian inheritance for some materialistic mirage. In either case, apostles are surrounded by the cold darkness of materialism and have urgent need to warm their hearts at the fire of God the Holy Spirit.

In order not to be caught in the current of indifferentism and atheism about them, apostles have to recall the immense burden that as other Christs they must take upon themselves. They must speak to God for the pagans to whom they minister, offering in their stead the thanksgiving which is the Creator's due for His gifts to all men. The compensating warmth of their own thanksgiving is best kindled by the contemplation of the greatest of all God's gifts to us, the gift of His love.

## Love Resides in the Will

We have heard and read so often that God loves each one of us individually that the tremendous tiding has lost the startling impact of news. But there is little excuse for this spiritual staleness here in China. In the joy of our newly baptized converts, we can see and feel as if for the first time the miracle of the Everlasting Love of God for each of the human beings He created.

God loved us from the first moment of our creation, or rather from the beginning of time when we were conceived in His mind. We have to become conscious of this truth in order to obtain a sane, balanced view of life. Otherwise we can discover no answer to the world's problems, or to the longings of our own hearts. Dorothy Day says in her autobiography that before she became a Catholic her religious ideas were of the vaguest sort. Nevertheless, her heart was crying out to God; and as she walked through the streets at night in her assignments in newspaper work, she kept repeating to herself over and over, "God loves me."

God's love is perduring. In the Book of Isaiah the Lord says, "Can a woman forget her infant, so as not to have pity on the son of her womb? And if she should forget, yet will I not forget thee" *(Isai. XLIX: 15)*. It is difficult to talk with others about God's love, because the manner in which we experience it and endeavor in our poor way to respond to it is our most intimate secret, a secret between each soul and its Creator. Words are so inadequate for the expression of this secret, that we dread to be misunderstood. Some of us are troubled when we do not experience an emotional love of God, but the lack of such spiritual consolation does not necessarily mean that our hearts have grown cold. It is true that divine love pierced the heart of St. Teresa of Avila, and she herself said that she was almost carried out of her senses by the ecstasy of pain. But that was a very unusual manifestation of the love between God and a human soul; and we are ordinary people.

Because God is invisible and intangible, He is loved by the will. How, then, can we love God? We know He loves us; how can we best love Him? This question reminds me of my mother, who died shortly after I entered the Maryknoll Foreign Mission Seminary.

She was the kind of person my numerous relatives used to seek out for advice. Sometimes, when my girl cousins were engaged, they used to say to my mother, "But I am not sure if I really love him. How can I tell if I love him enough to be with him the rest of my life?"

My mother would smile and answer, "You don't need to worry about that. You will grow to love him after you are married. The love that matters is the one that comes after the honeymoon blossoms have faded. You have all the rest of your life to love your husband."

## Give and Take

My mother's advice to the girls applies as much to divine love as to human love. We have all our lives to love God, and it need not be a matter of concern if we do not experience emotional love at any given time. To grow in the love of God, we need only to be always conscious of His presence and to show Him our affection by the will to please Him. It is a part of the law of give and take.

We must try to realize the wonder of God's love for us, because we are interested in those who single us out personally, not in those who slight us. Likewise, we are interested in those to whom we give ourselves and those we seek to benefit. In divine as well as in human relations, we have to feed our love by acts of love.

Words are not enough. Our Lord tells us that the man who says he loves God and does not prove it by the act of loving his neighbor is not of God. A married couple who call each other by endearing names, but do not perform reciprocal acts of thoughtfulness, will not grow in each other's love. Just as a priest is ordained forever, so the union between the Christian soul in the state of grace and God the Holy Spirit is for eternity. Therefore it is fatal to settle down into a routine, taking things for granted.

We must seek to grow in the knowledge of God, in order to increase our will to please Him by acts of love. Love presupposes knowledge. God made us to know

Him, to love Him, and to serve Him. We can begin to study Him by just looking at the ordinary things around us and saying to ourselves, this is from God. We have plenty of material to use in this elementary study of God, because we are completely surrounded by tokens of His love. Even after we have made progress in the spiritual life, it will not hurt us to continue this childlike method of learning to know God. St. Augustine, a great Doctor of the Church prayed: "Lord, that I may know Thee, and that I may know myself."

## Anchored in God's Love

Most of us belong to one or the other of two common types of character. There are persons who constantly seek appreciation, who become fainthearted and discouraged when praise and recognition are denied them. They feel a pressing need to be loved by others; and when they meet coldness, it hurts keenly. Persons of the other type of character are more concerned with pouring out their love and energies on others than with seeking affection for themselves. They spend themselves almost instinctively.

Both these sorts of persons are in peril in this world, and especially in pagan surroundings. Those who lean on others for affection will experience bitter disappointment, while souls who spend themselves on others without examination of the motive dissipate their energies. Both types of persons can succeed if they are anchored in the love of God, if the will to please Him impels their course of action. We must see and seek God in other human beings. The alternative is moral shipwreck.

God gave us His love and He also gave us a free will, so that we might be able to direct all the energies of our being to loving Him in return. To love any creature apart from the Creator is to debase and abuse the gift of free will. Only in God can the love we all need be satisfied and find a safe outlet. Come, Holy Spirit, Light of the soul, that we may see in all creatures the glowing beauty of God's love.

## Five

# Be Thou Our Best Consolation

Modern pagans, who have closed their souls to the tremendous significance of the truth that God is Love, and who are seeking only sensible pleasures here and now, have debased and weakened the interpretation of the word "love." The newspapers and novels of today often portray love as something very emotional, spineless, and mawkish, consisting wholly of enjoyment and pleasure. Even Catholics have been insensibly affected by this degeneration in concept. We have only to recall the cloying sentimentality of certain modern representations of the Sacred Heart of Jesus, and then to compare them with the strength of the graciously serene medieval statue of the Beautiful God at the Cathedral of Amiens.

If we examine our own hearts sincerely, we realize that even in human relations, we love and admire people because of their fortitude, firmness, and constancy. True love is not weakening; it casts out weakness and fear.

As for the union of love binding the soul of the faithful Christian to God the Holy Spirit, it is stronger than death.

So that when we call God's Love our best consolation, we have to eliminate any mawkish idea of seeking sympathy in our weakness. The real meaning of the word "console" is to consolidate, to strengthen, to make taut; and this meaning fits in with the true definition of love. "I can do all things in Him Who strengtheneth me" *(Phil. IV: 13)*. Love puts a heart in us; it does not debilitate us. A person truly in love can never be a coward. Forgetful of self, he acts fearlessly for the one he loves. He sometimes even attempts impossibilities.

At times, sympathy not only is not true consolation; but it is misplaced. When a person is sick, for example, he doesn't want sympathy so much as strength. That is probably why most nurses and doctors are hard-boiled. They are firm and they hand you a bitter dose with a smile. That is also probably one reason why medicines are bitter and distasteful. If they were sweet and palatable, we would be inclined to become hypochondriacs, leaning on them.

It is because love is fortifying that God often sends it to us in the shape of suffering. When a blacksmith takes a bar of iron and heats it in the fire until it is red hot, his purpose is not to weaken the metal. Rather, he plunges the glowing bar into cold water, to make it hard as steel. Gold, also, is tried by fire and fortified. In like manner,

God strengthens us by sending us sickness and other so-called misfortunes.

## An Ancient Form of Prayer

In meditating on God's love for us, formalized prayer often seems inadequate. Long before St. Ignatius formalized prayer in meditations and spiritual exercises, the old Irish monks for centuries were accustomed to the litany form of prayer; and I am attracted to that ancient way of talking to God. The Church approves of it also, incorporating many litanies into her worship.

In Old Testament days, the Psalmist gave utterance to his love and worship of God in interjections and exclamatory phrases such as we use in our litanies. It is an age-long way of prayer and I think it suits our limited minds. Few of us are theologians, trained to make a thesis and define it in all its parts. The natural way of thought suits us best, even if it is often disjointed.

A person in love does not write to the beloved in formalized, logical sentences. In fact, if he were to read over his own love letters years later, he would wonder how he could have ever thought such a mass of exclamations and superlatives made sense. If it is so difficult to give logical expression to our love of another human being, what wonder that there is some incoherence when we try to speak of the love of God. We find ourselves repeating the cry of Jeremiah: "Ah, ah, ah, Lord God, behold, I cannot speak, for I am a child" *(Jer. I: 6).*

The very Pentecostal Sequence we are now considering is a series of ejaculations to God the Holy Spirit, invoking His love for us under one of its wonderful manifestations after another. Because our minds are limited, it is helpful to us to consider one at a time the surpassing attributes of the Spirit of Love. The litany form of prayer is a splendid way of talking to God as we walk on the road ministering to members of our church of the wayside, or watch the stars from the deck of some river junk. Our hearts are filled with new praises of the Trinity and of the Blessed Virgin; it is the poetry in the Catholic Church.

## Real Love Makes Demands

So, today, we are praying to God the Holy Spirit and are speaking His praises as our Consoler, our Strengthener. The fire in His love will burn out our sinful weaknesses, so that we may cooperate with Him in renewing the face of the earth. We seek to become partners of the Spirit of Love.

Before I entered Maryknoll, I was often condemned to a distasteful task. At dances, my very charitable sister would ask me to rescue the "wallflowers" and waltz them around. It was easy to see why most of those girls were not asked to dance. They did not act like partners, but like clinging vines. We do not want to take the role of clinging vines in our union with Him Who gives us abundant strength to become co-workers with God.

God the Holy Spirit comes to us in all the sacraments of the Church, to strengthen us for our partnership with Him. In the reception of several of the sacraments, we are anointed with oil, because in all ages athletes preparing for a contest were rubbed down with oil to strengthen them and to limber them up. There is nothing debilitating or enervating in the unction of the Holy Spirit. It is bracing, tingling, and, in a sense, painful.

The unction of the Holy Spirit is painful, because it tautens our flabby spiritual muscles. His love makes difficult demands on us. Father Price, the Co-Founder of Maryknoll, used to say often: "If you are not struggling, there is something wrong; you are going back." This struggling in partnership with God the Holy Spirit does not imply sadness or worry; His anointing strengthens us, so that with joy we run as swift athletes to do his bidding.

## The Sacred Secret

It would be well for us to ask ourselves from time to time what has been our attitude toward the hardships that are inevitable in earthly life—sickness, heavy responsibilities, disappointments, and mental strain of various kinds. We know that in His love for us, God is giving us an opportunity to partake in our small way in the redemptive sufferings of His Divine Son; yet we often shrink back from the ordeal. Perhaps we have frequently sought "consolation," in the pagan sense of rushing to others to seek their sympathy.

Recently I read a story in which the heroine always resisted the temptation to talk about her trials. "No, I cannot afford to spend it," she would say; and no one knew what she was talking about. The fact is that as soon as we lean on other human beings for consolation, we have spent our energy; we have not saved it for the service of God. We are like a wife who tattle-tales every time she has a disagreement with her husband. She takes all the sacredness out of the union with her husband by seeking sympathy elsewhere. If God gives us suffering, it is a sacred secret between Him and our souls, and not a matter for complaint to others.

The right acceptance of suffering, physical or mental, does not mean that we must not have recourse to legitimate remedies. We have to employ common sense in the use of remedies, without forgetting that suffering is inevitable and part of God's plan for us. If we do not permit God's love to test and strengthen us by the exercise of our fortitude in suffering, then we fail Him, and that is cowardice in the spiritual life. We are shirkers, shrinking away from the hand of God.

Another sort of spiritual cowardice is pessimism, always seeing the dark side of life. Some priests return from a mission trip with the glowing zeal of the first Apostles, rejoicing that they have cast out demons from pagan souls in the Name of Christ. Others can describe the same experiences and make them sound like a series of calamities. There is an even more objectionable form of pessimism, manifested by those who always try to throw cold water on the enthusiasm of others. These are the Job's comforters, who instinctively doubt the feasibility of a plan, always worry about future possibilities, and are in general hangers of black crepe. Once in a while, we are all apt to see the dark side of things; but we must recognize this shrinking from life as a temptation.

## A Perfect Partnership

Our fight is against the princes and the powers of darkness, and the devil seeks to distract and weaken us in the fray by insidious temptations to moral cowardice. He whispers to us that we are alone, misunderstood, and that our burden is too heavy to carry. Yet, all the while, God the Holy Spirit is simply trying to test us, to save us, and to sanctify us to a degree where He can find something in us to admire. The Holy Spirit does not withhold His yearning love, in the form of mercy, even from sinners; but He gives the love of friendship only to those who seek to become saints.

In earthly love, we can imagine qualities in ourselves and in others. We do not have to imagine qualities in God, because we know that He is Charity, the perfect form of goodness; God does not imagine qualities in us, because he knows the inmost secrets of the souls He created. So He gives us a chance to become, not merely His servants, but His friends, even though His grace has to go nine tenths of the way to meet our feeble response.

That is the union of love in which the faithful Christian dwells in God. We admire His Goodness, and He admires our receptiveness. It is a partnership of the Creator with the souls He made in His image and likeness, and hence capable of returning His love. When the thought of our trials tempts us to self-pity, we can turn to God the Holy Spirit, our best consolation, our true strength, the real partner who always nurses us along with a firm hand and gives us the medicine we need.

Our Divine Partner does not yield to our whimperings and complaints. His consolations take the form of a fortifying grace that will enable us to be tried as it were by fire. He is seeking to make our love for Him like His own, stronger than death. It is a perfect partnership, in which God the Holy Spirit burns away the dross of our souls, in order that we may live forever in the joy of contemplating the Purity of the Triune God.

## Six

# Dwell as Loving Guest in Our Hearts

As children, we are taught the etiquette of receiving guests. Last night I was discussing with the Chinese students in our hostel the varying customs of hospitality in different lands. Chinese hospitality is more indiscriminate than ours. When a man comes on business to a Chinese home, he is offered tea, tobacco, and even invited to remain for a meal. It would not be a matter for surprise, if the master of the home extended his hospitality to the chance business acquaintance with an invitation to spend the night.

In Western countries, we are more exacting. We pick and choose our friends, and distinguish between friends and acquaintances. Whenever we do invite a person to our house, it is a mark of special friendship. We try to anticipate his needs, and to treat him even better than those who live in the home. So we Westerners should have a clear appreciation of the joy of offering hospitality to a cherished guest.

When we invoke God the Holy Spirit under the name of Loving Guest of the soul, we take a special look at the quality of our own hospitality. In the ceremony of the consecration of a bishop, hospitality is repeatedly emphasized. It is supposed to be the special mark of a bishop. I find this episcopal hospitality the most difficult virtue of all to cultivate over here in China; and it must be harder still for bishops in the United States, who are hemmed in by all sorts of duties not required of missionary prelates. Yet, no bishop really lives up to his office unless he is hospitable.

Hospitality should also be the special mark of all superiors and, indeed, of all missioners. It is one of the striking paradoxes of Catholic missionary life that the apostle must, at one and the same time, remain absorbed in God and dedicate himself to a life of hospitality. From the first century of Christianity, this has been true of all missionary work. All religious institutes have found that when they are undertaking missionary work, they have to assume a new character. When St. Ignatius started his great Society of Jesus, it would have appeared normal if he had kept his pioneer Jesuits together for a number of years in order to establish a spirit of union in the infant institute. Instead of that, the missionary vocation of the Jesuits led their Founder to disperse his earliest followers. St. Francis Xavier made his novitiate in the Far East; he was finally received into the Society of Jesus by mail; and for long years he was not certain who had been elected first Father General of the Jesuits.

So, the missioner who lives up to his vocation has to be especially adaptable. The contradictions in our life are all part of God's plan for us. Hours spent in the chapel are not the only means of entertaining the Beloved Guest of the soul. We can often please Him better when we are out in the highways and byways of China, offering to needy souls the hospitality of our Christian love.

## Lonely but Not Lonesome

No one is as lonely as a missioner in a pagan country. I say lonely, not lonesome. There is a big difference; and the zealous missioner is not lonesome, because he is always ready with his hospitality. He is constantly in the company of other human beings, yet he lacks real companionship because these people have nothing in common with his own ideals. Out of love for God, he has given up social intercourse with fellow Christians. He is lonely, because he has given himself completely to the work of welcoming these strangers into his Father's Home.

I often think how it was with St. Francis Xavier on his frequent ocean voyages. There would be three or four hundred passengers and crew members, and often he would be the only priest aboard. The members of the crew were mostly adventurers "on the make," or jailbirds afloat because they were trying to escape the police. In many cases, the passengers were of equally unsavory character.

When there was a good wind, the crew joined the passengers in gambling, drinking, and swearing. If any man were ever lonely, St. Francis Xavier was during those voyages. At the same time, he was the least lonesome of all those aboard. The loving hospitality he offered the souls of these rough men drew them like a magnet. On his deathbed, many a derelict joyfully accepted the saint's welcome to the long-forgotten road to heaven.

All missioners experience something of the same loneliness felt by St. Francis Xavier. We look down from a mountaintop on a teeming Chinese city or prosperous village, and know that it does not contain one baptized soul who would share our Christian ideals. But our very loneliness acts as a spur, urging us on to invite these pagan strangers to brotherhood with us in the Mystical Body of Christ.

## A Special Problem

Of course, even when Catholic priests and Sisters are living in a Christian country and surrounded by numerous members of their own religious institute, they can be very much alone. Each of us is an individual. Other human beings cannot wholly penetrate our thoughts; and we, in turn, are unable to express our thoughts fully to others. There is an innate citadel of the soul that fellow human beings cannot take by assault, so that the companionship of men never relieves our innermost loneliness.

On the missions, in addition to the loneliness experienced at times by all human hearts, we have a special problem resulting from the inability to pick and choose those to whom we must offer the hospitality of our friendship. We are in a small house with one or two confreres, and kinks in our hospitable charity are apt to appear.

When I entered Maryknoll in 1912, there were only six of us pioneer students. I had been in a college of several hundred ordinary men students; and we got along beautifully, with never a quarrel among the lot of us. I could not understand why the few of us at Maryknoll, all supposed to be potential saints, squabbled in small ways from sunrise to sunset. There were about a dozen jobs for the six of us to cover, and we were constantly crossing lines. We were supposed to be more mature men than the college boys we had left behind us; but here we were, finding it harder to live together.

At first it shocked me, but then I realized that in college we could select congenial companions. If I didn't like a boy I was not obliged to rub elbows with him;

and I naturally went round with those with whom I had something in common. These conditions did not put my charity to the test.

On the missions, we are apt to have even fewer companions than the six pioneers of the infant Maryknoll. We cannot always find congenial social intercourse to soothe nerves taut from bickerings with the companions it is impossible to escape. A little reflection will show us that most of our uncharitable thoughts, harshness, and coldness here on the missions are due to irritation with the one or two daily associates whose company cannot be avoided.

## Bound to Greater Hospitality

The Christian who, for one reason or another, has only limited opportunities of human intercourse is bound to greater hospitality because of that very fact. If his companion has no one but him with whom to recreate and exchange ideas, then the warmth of his welcome must glow with unfailing charity.

Here in China, we missioners are the only representatives of the Divine Interest in our Christians and in the other sheep who are not yet of Christ's fold. We cannot escape the duty of welcoming those who come to us with a charity reflecting the indwelling in our own souls of the Holy Spirit, the Spirit of Love. It is not easy to extend this welcome to all alike, because it is human nature to be critical of others.

A while ago, I was watching the cook at the hostel while he put a new chicken he had bought in with the others. Every other chicken came over and gave the poor, forlorn newcomer a peck. Finally the wretched creature admitted its inferiority by standing on one leg in a corner with drooping feathers, and the others left it alone. We have to be aware of a tendency in ourselves to act like these chickens. We size newcomers up and give them a peck to see how they can stand it. It is the animal in all of us.

Before St. Francis Borgia joined the Society of Jesus, he had been a great noble, accustomed to being served constantly. Unconsciously, he began bossing his Jesuit confreres around; and many of them must have felt like pecking at the pride of this overbearing newcomer. But St. Ignatius knew how to extend the hospitality of his charity to his new subject, destined to become one of the glories of the Society. He assigned two Jesuits to serve the highborn novice; and then the shamed St. Francis Borgia realized how incongruous it was to have servants in the religious life.

Of course, in the case of some new acquaintances, we are hard put to discover faults to criticize. When I was a student at Maryknoll, a wealthy young lady joined the Sisters' community. I recall seeing her arrive in her own fine automobile. The first task assigned to the new postulant by the Mother Foundress was to serve dinner to her chauffeur. The young lady performed this service with such simple and spontaneous hospitality, that the chauffeur ceased to feel his initial embarrassment. It is not difficult to open our hearts to people like this young lady; but we must be ready, too, with the patient, discerning charity of St. Ignatius.

## Hospitality of the Heart

Older priests often find it hard to overlook the trying ways of new curates; and I say this from the fullness of long personal experience. The young priests appear much too casual in their assumption that everything on the premises is for their own convenience, and that anything lacking will be forthwith supplied. We see the defects in our companions very keenly; but I fear that often those same shortcomings are going to register against us ourselves, not them. If we had been more ready with our understanding sympathy, we could have helped the newcomers to erase the brashness of inexperience.

Some of us do not own a house in which to welcome guests; but we can always offer to those seeking friendship the hospitality of our heart. In heaven, we shall be known by our response to the fellow beings who knocked at the door of our heart. When we are cold to others, disdain them, and wound them with sharp criticism, then we are shutting both them and Christ out of our heart.

When hospitality of the heart seems hard to offer, we can inflame our charity by recalling the words Our Lord will speak to the just on the Day of Judgment: "I was a stranger, and you took Me in. . . . As long as you did it to one of these my least brethren, you did it to Me" *(Matt. XXV: 35–40).*

## Receiving God in Others

We invoke the Third Person of the Blessed Trinity with longing, as the Loving Guest of the soul; but do we always recognize Him, when He comes to us in other creatures and in the daily circumstances of our lives? If, like St. Francis Xavier, we strove to see God in every person, every creature, every happening, every message, every duty, we could never be alone, much less lonesome.

As we recall that other human beings are actual or possible "temples of the Holy Spirit," we cannot but love them in Him. When we perceive God in the person we are talking with, we cannot be cold or disdainful or uncharitable. If we find God along the paths of our life's journey, we cannot give way to lonely discouragement, because our innate desire for companionship is richly satisfied.

Come, Loving Guest of the soul! He comes to us under myriad disguises; and unless we are always on the watch to receive Him, we may lose much of the joy of His divine companionship. But for those who have gained awareness of the Holy Spirit in all the sensible universe, visiting with the Beloved Guest of their soul is an ever renewed delight. They receive the strengthening consolation that otherwise men are driven to seek vainly outside of God. They have found Him Whom their soul loves, and He has set in order charity in them. They hold Him, and they will not let Him go.

## Seven

# Come, Divine Renewer

In all her prayers to God the Holy Spirit, the Church seems to emphasize especially His love of renewing the face of the earth. He grants a refreshment and a new start to what is right and just. He is the Eternal Giver, and when monotony has jaded the zeal of our spiritual striving, we can turn with perfect confidence to Him as the Divine Renewer. St. Paul has told us that "the charity of God is poured forth in our hearts by the Holy Spirit, Who is given us" *(Rom. V: 5).*

Sometimes it seems to us that our spiritual efforts have reached a sort of dead end, and we are tempted by weary discouragement. We have been depending too much on our human efforts to grow in the love of God. The fact is that only the Holy Spirit, by communicating Himself to the soul in the inpouring of divine charity, can raise it up to the love of friendship with God. Then we are empowered to love God with an affection which is divine in its principle. We have put on Christ. Come, Divine Renewer of our souls!

## Heaven on Earth

In our youth, God called us to serve Him in some particular walk of life. We answered the call generously, and knew a period like heaven on earth. We saw God's truth and His way and His purpose with the eyes of innocence. This was the true view of life, and it is good to remember it. More than this, we can ask the Holy Spirit with confidence to renew the youth of our soul.

When the Maryknoll pioneers arrived in China, they had no clear conception of the task ahead; but they were eager to undertake anything they were asked to do. As a student I once went to look at the Anglican Cathedral in New York City. The old Anglican verger knew that I and the other Maryknollers with me would eventually be assigned to the foreign missions. He told us that their missioners tried out the mission life in the field during three years before they decided to continue in it. When he heard that we were to have no such period of testing the foreign apostolate, he said he thought it was unfair that we bind ourselves for life to a work virtually unknown to us.

We, of course, made light of the misgivings of our kind acquaintance, because our dedication was whole-souled. We landed in China ready for anything. If we had been told it was necessary to live on one meal a day, well, we would have made a try of it. If we had been warned that we would be insulted and mocked and stoned, we would have been willing to bear witness for Christ, because then we clearly saw the work as it truly is, a divine continuation of His own apostolate.

## The Dull Gray of Monotony

The bane of life on the missions, and in all other walks of life, is monotony. When we begin to settle down, and everything becomes monochromi—a dull gray—it is time to call a halt and stop for refreshment. A whirlwind round of activity and recreation is not the remedy for the grayness of monotony; no man experiences this bane more acutely than the one who never takes time to think in his heart.

The mere repetition of daily events does not necessarily bring on the blight of monotony; it comes rather from the staleness of our own spirit. The repetition of the prayers of the Rosary can result in vapid distractions. But for the person who repeats the prayers while meditating on the Blessed Trinity and the Mother of God, the Rosary is a wonderful means of uplifting and refreshing the soul.

Fortunately, God in His mercy makes it easy for us to forget past weariness of the spirit and the sad days of our lives. A brief season of refreshment, and invigorated by the Divine Renewer, we are ready for a new start. I recall that when I returned to the United States for a decennial visit, I had not been five minutes on the boat before I forgot the cares and difficulties of my life as a Mission Superior. I saw things afresh from God's viewpoint, and I was full of apostolic eagerness to take up my work again.

## A Subtle Temptation

The thought of the virtue of perseverance is apt to evoke a forbidding image in the minds of the young. It suggests a long, taxing struggle until old age and death; and most of us don't like to think of ourselves as getting old. Long ago in the desert, St. Anthony of Egypt knew how difficult it was to look forward to a lifetime of perseverance, so he told his novices just to concentrate on one day at a time. But if it is hard to look forward to the virtue of perseverance, I can tell you from personal experience that it looks marvelous when viewed in reverse, from the vantage of advancing years.

It might be thought that apostles, of all people, should find perseverance easy because of the very nature of their work. We know in our hearts that our work is the most thrilling in the world, the battle for souls against the dark hosts of Evil. But the human weakness of all of us alike is such that we missioners sometimes find even the apostolate drably wearisome; and a restless craving for change sets in.

We may tire of our field of labor, and say to ourselves that we could accomplish more for God and souls in Africa than in China. This, of course, is an illusion. In the eyes of God, human souls have the same value, whatever part of the world may happen to be their earthly habitation. Perhaps we look with envy on other mission fields where the harvest of souls is abundant; but most of us have been consoled with more converts than was Our Lord and Master in Palestine.

After a while, we may feel that our zeal is cramped by outdated mission methods in use in our territory; and we chafe under the direction of superiors who seem to be moving in a narrow rut. A little more experience of the people's ways and a better understanding of their traditional mode of life will show us that the innovations we envisioned could have led only to disaster.

Again, the tedium of our days appears to be the result of living in close quarters with uncongenial companions. We think our associates lack vision and that their interests are of the most pedestrian nature. Yet, when we were in the seminary with these same men and hundreds of other classmates, those we now consider dullards may have excited our warm enthusiasm.

It is necessary to realize that when a drab staleness saps our spiritual energies, we are undergoing a subtle temptation to which all human beings are exposed. The fault does not lie primarily in our work, our surroundings, or our companions; but in our own restless hearts. Come, Divine Renewer and refresh with the fire of Thy zeal our jaded wills!

## A Sign of Victory

A great consolation in the midst of our bouts with the gray of monotony is that the devil finds it worth his while to tempt us. If we were not achieving a measure of success in our work for God and souls, the evil one would not waste his time on us. He is trying to unsettle and distract us, so that we will lack the courage to persevere until the end.

Young Americans are especially vulnerable to temptation by drab monotony, because in our country today youth is brought up on excitement and novelty. A great change in this respect has taken place since my own childhood.

At home in the evenings, we sat around a big table and quietly studied, while my father wrote articles for his newspapers. My mother was often busy with the mending for our large family; but at other times she, too, was engaged in literary work. It was understood that none of us would retire before my father led the quite lengthy family night prayers. We loved our evenings at home, and did not hanker after exciting amusement.

When I was last in the United States, I saw how my nephew spent his evenings. He rushed home, threw his cap in a corner, and did not begin to study his lessons until he had the radio going full blast. His parents bore the din patiently. My nephew would find it much harder than I did to enjoy evenings in a Chinese village, with only a candle to read by, and no companions other than my Breviary and the silent stars.

If young American apostles have to fight harder to overcome monotony's temptation to stale discouragement, then their victory will taste all the sweeter when they turn for refreshment to their union with God the Holy Spirit, the Divine Renewer. Our first Mission Superior, Father Price of holy memory, had a heroic remedy for the wounds of monotony. "When you find anything monotonous," he would say, "keep at it five or ten minutes longer."

## Renewing the Face of the Earth

Our vocation is to cooperate with the Holy Spirit in renewing the face of the earth; and we cannot be effective partners of God when we drag along with flagging energies. At such times, our Divine Co-Worker is ready to restore our joy and our strength; but He wishes us first to react against monotony with an effort of our own will. There are all sorts of remedies for monotony. One is to put more of ourselves into our apostolate, to seek out new ways of presenting the truths of religion to our catechumens. Our people will be moved by homely little illustrations taken from their own daily lives and surroundings; and we will take fresh interest in the work because of the personal effort we have put into it.

The good worker in any walk of life is never the resigned drudge. Drudgery is doing the right thing in the wrong way, or seeing it from the wrong viewpoint. When we are leading a life of drudgery, there is something wrong in ourselves. Either our will or our understanding or our imagination needs to be refreshed.

Too often, we do not actively will to accomplish our apostolic duties, but tackle them merely because they are on the schedule. A real effort to understand and know our people can frequently suffice in itself to render our work once more vivid and exciting. As for the missioner who uses his imagination, he can tramp over weary miles little aware of physical discomfort, because he is rejoicing in the infinitely varied beauty of God in the created universe.

Our recurring need of pauses for spiritual refreshment makes me think of the little tea houses on our Hakka mountaintops. They were placed there years ago by Chinese Buddhists, to restore the strength of wayfaring messengers, pilgrims, and poets. We pause, in our turn, at the welcome mountain refuges from weariness. Under the cool shade of a tree, we sip the invigorating drink; and out of the monotonous glare of the sun, our eyes are rested. We look down into the valley and see things again in their proper perspective and normal color. In the same way, it is good and natural for wayfarers on life's journey to pause in their toil, for refreshment. If we take our refreshment in God the Holy Spirit, looking to Him for the living water that renews the strength of the soul, then He will help us view our work from a height infinitely more revealing than the loftiest mountaintop.

We will perceive how glorious is our work for souls, and how immediately united it is with the symbolic death of Our Lord at Holy Mass. Though the central act of the Sacrifice of the Mass is the same every day, Holy Mother the Church excites our interest by constantly varying the accidentals of the liturgy. In like manner, restoring our souls in God the Holy Spirit, the Divine Renewer, we must rouse ourselves to cooperate with Him in ever fresh ways in re-creating the face of the earth.

## Eight

# Be Thou Our Rest in Toil

The Holy Spirit not only renews our strength during pauses in our work; He is also our Rest while we are laboring. Too many of us are like Martha when she received our Lord into her home; we are incessantly "careful and troubled about many things." Jesus loved Martha with special tenderness for her solicitous service of Him; and so He was the more desirous that she should learn how, at the same time, to work and to rest in God.

When people visit a religious institute, they sometimes wonder if much work is being done. They see everyone going about and looking contented, but they would like to know what is being actually accomplished. When I myself joined Maryknoll, I did not at first think that Father Founder was very busy. We students used to see him going about the grounds, seemingly carefree and with a brief case under his arm. We excused his apparent inaction by saying that every job can afford one boss, at least one man who doesn't have to work!

Then there was our Co-Founder, Father Price. He seemed to take his time about everything, even about his meals. Our initial impression was that he had nothing to do all day, except to pray. Even when the Mother Foundress of the Maryknoll Sisters filled in as our cook during the frequent desertions of the hired help, she did not appear to be working very hard. She would whip up a salad or a dessert in no time, and seemingly without effort. Of course, all of us pioneers have long since understood that these builders of Maryknoll were carrying on tremendous work, and at the same time resting in God the Holy Spirit.

## Sham Activity

In organized labor outside of religious institutions, there is a lot of sham and bluff. Before he joined Maryknoll, one of our pioneer students worked for some months as a day laborer on a construction job. His particular task was to fill a wheelbarrow and push it up a hill. At the end of the first day, he was politely told by the boss of the union that he must not work so hard. He was creating an unhealthy competition, and there was danger that the same amount of work might be demanded from others.

The future Maryknoller accordingly slowed down, but that did not please the boss either. "No, you must not seem to be making fewer trips up the hill," that worthy said. "You are packing your wheelbarrow too full. Just pack it loosely, and carry half the weight each trip." So, our confrere had to conform to the regulations of the union if he wanted to stay on the job.

In our apostolic work, of course, we do not have to perform superfluous motion to please a union boss. But we can do a lot of bustling around and undergo unneccessary nervous strain, if our effort is primarily to please some mission superior or the Ordinary of our diocese. At that, we may not be making the hoped-for impression. The experienced superior is not deceived by wasted motion.

The only boss of our labors for souls is God; and unless we keep this wonderful thought constantly in mind, we cannot do really efficient work. How thankful we ought to be that we do not have to bluff. We are working for a Divine Master, Who sees us all the time, but Who does not expect of us impossibilities. God is able to gauge exactly our capacities; and He wants us to rest during our labor, to rest in Him.

## Where Sanity Lies

Many of us have heard the story of the New Yorker who was explaining to an Oriental visitor how improved subway connections would soon permit him to arrive in his downtown office five minutes earlier. The Oriental seemed mildly surprised at his host's enthusiasm. "And what will you do during the extra five minutes?" he wondered. The New Yorker had given no thought to that.

In work for souls, and especially here in the Orient, we have to measure our activity not by our own restlessness, but by the needs of other people, who may often keep us waiting. Instead of fretting ourselves into nervous worry over hours of apparent inactivity, we can find in rest in God the Holy Spirit the peace of soul necessary for planning new and better mission methods. God seldom gives us inspirations when we are caught up in whirlwind activity; we are more apt to form fertile plans for His service during some long wait under the stars on a stalled river junk.

When I was young I had a very dear friend, much older than I was, who had spent seventeen years in various British prisons. He was a political prisoner, because of his efforts for Irish independence. He told me that for most of the inmates, the hardest part of prison life was not the work. They found the four or five hours of waiting, of inactivity between signals, the most difficult of all. Some of the men became almost insane with the nervous fret, the irritation of not being able to do what they wanted to do. Others sank into a sort of apathetic sleep; they vegetated almost without thinking at all.

My friend, on the contrary, kept sane and cheerful by looking forward to the hours of waiting, instead of dreading their approach. He was rather grateful to the British Government for providing him with such a splendid opportunity to think things out, to clarify his thoughts, and to orientate himself. In short, he was confident that God blessed his painful labors. So he rested in the Holy Spirit during times of seeming inactivity, periods in reality of especially fruitful advancement of the cause of Irish freedom.

## The Integrated Christian Life

The full Christian life requires that we pass all our hours, those of labor and of rest, in union with God. If our work is worrying us until we are irritable with nervous strain, then we are not combining it properly with rest in the Holy Spirit. If our rest is taken apart from God, as a scatterbrained recreation without creative thought, then it is wrong and misplaced. The Christian must not give himself too much either to work or to rest; he can find perfect balance only in seeking both in union with God.

Soon after I had entered the Maryknoll Seminary, I began to fear that I was, perhaps, too introspective a type for the mission life. I went to Father Founder and told him how hard it was for me to try to hustle around. "Well, much of our work is invisible and intangible," said Father Walsh reassuringly. "You cannot measure it by human means; and sometimes a period of quiet reflection will accomplish more for the good of the Church than if the time had been spent in outward activity."

Of course, Father Founder did not mean to commend thought that does not produce action. The dreamer without actions is certainly an unprofitable servant. Only in God, Who is Perfection, can our lopsided human natures be rounded out into the integral Christian life.

In itself, human activity cannot be free of strain, because of our very effort to overcome our limitations. Only the activity of God is an infinite repose, because He is Absolute, Infinite, Life Itself, He Who Is. By merging our little strivings and our rest in our union with the Holy Spirit, the Fount of Life, we can find a peace that is a foretaste of heaven.

# Nine

# Sanctify Our Passions

Our passions are God-given, and good in themselves. They enable us to enjoy life, to appreciate things, and to make continued effort. In fact, we would be paralyzed creatures if we were without passions. In the Apocalypse, the Spirit of God voices a terrible condemnation of those lukewarm men who are afraid of strong emotions, who are neither hot nor cold *(Apoc. III: 16).*

In the derivation of our English word "passion," the idea of suffering is implied. The intensity, the heat, of an emotion causes pain. Only the fire of the charity of the Holy Spirit can control the fire of our human passions, directing them to joy in the intense effort to please God. The Passion of Our Lord Jesus Christ redeemed the world; and all the years of His earthly life He desired ardently to drink the chalice of suffering which would be given Him by His Heavenly Father. The passions of men, when they are lit by self-interest and are not purified and supernaturalized by the fire of the Holy Spirit, often destroy both body and soul.

## We Are Not Pure Spirits

We can think of our passions as the motive powers of our being, given to us by God to keep us alive. The desire of life in a sick person is a doctor's best ally in curing his patient. Our passions impel us toward some real or imaginary good. When they are supernaturalized, they give us zest in accomplishing the things that are pleasing to God. In our prayer, when we beg God the Holy Spirit to give us a relish, a hunger, an appetizing taste for what is good and right, we are speaking in terms of passions. Our Lord Himself, in the Sermon on the Mount, spoke of those who hunger and thirst after justice.

So, we must not get a horror of the passions. Buddhism fell into this error, teaching that nirvana, the absence of all passions, is the state of eternal bliss. In the third century of the Christian Era, this same error led to the heresy of the Manichees. In a modified form, this mistake has plagued some Christians through the centuries. They tend to consider the natural faculties of the body as evil in themselves, forgetting that by virtue of Our Lord's Resurrection, the souls of the just will eventually be reunited to their glorified bodies in heaven. God did not create us as pure spirits.

## When Props Are Removed

Writers on the spiritual life say that it is a peculiar temptation of those in religious institutes to try to live on a wholly spiritual plane, taking no care of the body. But like all humans, religious are made up of matter and spirit. If they try to live as angels, they will sooner or later be reminded in painful ways that they are still in the flesh.

It is true that in the novitiate and the seminary our passions are placed under an outside control. The rules and regulations, the surveillance of superiors, and the study of holy things insulate us from uncontrolled sensations, so that we come to think of the passions as something outside our ordinary plan of life. Our passions may, in fact, have become so dormant that we are not sure which of them is the predominant one.

Then, some fine day, the props of the novitiate or the seminary are removed, and we suddenly discover that the passions are very much with us. We find ourselves yielding to sensations of impatience, jealousy, sadness, and dislike for certain people; and we hastily conclude that our spiritual progress had suffered a serious setback. Actually it hasn't. It is just that we are now on our own, and must seek a clearer understanding of the fact that the passions are the stuff of which both sinners and saints are made.

## Learning to See Aright

In thinking about our passions, there are many angles from which we should consider them. Passions, of course, are powers of the sensitive body; but in human beings they are also rational, because they are more or less governed by the will. When passion in a human being becomes so disorderly it is beyond the control of the will, then that man or woman sinks to the level of an animal. Animal rage, for example, can lead to quite involuntary, irrational murder.

Our passions are affected by environment, heredity, and health. The man who acts like a saint in church can give way to violent temper as soon as he returns to vexations in his own home or office. People of the Nordic races are not given to using a stiletto on the least provocation; but they nurse a cold, sullen hatred longer than volatile peoples from the South. Bursts of anger may be due to a headache; and jealousy is often caused by physical weakness.

God Who made us knows what is in us. So, also, we who in Christ have become the adopted sons of God must withhold judgment of the passions of others and be patient with ourselves. "Charity is patient, is kind, . . . thinketh no evil" *(I Cor. XIII: 4–5)*. Only the fire of the charity of the Holy Spirit can so temper and purify our passions that in His light we can learn to see aright.

## Like a Woolen Sock

Another useful little point to know about the passions is that when we give way to any one of them, we are yielding to all of them. To realize this makes us a bit less self-complacent. The passions are like a woolen sock, all knit together. When they become unraveled in one place, a tangled snarl soon follows. On the other hand, if we concentrate on controlling our predominant passion, we will at the same time control all the rest of them.

Sometimes we fool ourselves so often about our predominant passion that we excuse it in ourselves more readily than some other less frequent excess. Suddenly, we discover that we have a sharp tongue and we are much ashamed of it; but perhaps sarcasm is not our predominant failing, after all. The predominant passion is deeply rooted, and the only way it can be effectively faced is in our daily examination of conscience. It is the one sin that is constantly weakening and loosening our spiritual life. If we give way to envy frequently, for example, we are also yielding to pride, sadness, and impatience. So, if we can control our dominant passion, all the rest will fall into their proper places.

When we find ourselves yielding constantly to an uncontrolled passion, perhaps we are not faithful or sufficiently thorough in our daily examination of conscience. We can often be blind to our predominant passion, when all our companions are well aware of it. For this reason, the nicknames our familiars bestow on us can be very revealing. If our friends call us Lazy Bones, it will not be leaping at conclusions to surmise that we are giving way rather constantly to sloth. So, occasionally, it does not hurt us to heed what others think of us.

## Portraying Christ

Most of all, we need the light of God the Holy Spirit in the effort to discover our predominant passion, and then in the striving to temper its heat and to supernaturalize it. He will also moderate our impatience, so that we will not be cast down by the consciousness of our weaknesses.

It seems to me that we ought to examine ourselves on sadness as thoroughly and as frequently as on any other weakness. Too often we substitute sadness for repentance. Then, instead of correcting the weakness that is troubling us, we are yielding to yet another one. Irregulated, unruly sadness can become a predominant passion, and one that can all but extinguish the joy a Christian should have in God.

Natural motives for controlling our passions, such as the desire to be considered a gentleman, are good in so far as they form correction in us. But the Christian can invoke an incomparably higher motive, because his task is to portray Christ to the world. The charity of God the

Holy Spirit will inflame our zeal in the task of effacing the ugly shadows cast by our unruly passions on our portrayal of the Divine Likeness.

## Ten

# Grant Us Thy Solace in Adversity

God the Holy Spirit, the Spirit of Love, is our solace in grief and adversity. We all have our griefs, and often it is difficult for our fellow human beings to sympathize with us. That is because grief is very relative and personal. What tears at the heart of one person can seem a quite trivial matter even to his closest friends. Only the love of God fathoms the secrets of our human hearts and knows when we are most in need of comfort. More than that, the Holy Spirit makes us feel the purifying power of grief accepted in the spirit of Christ.

St. Peter had no clear understanding of his Master's work and of his own future vocation until his eyes had been washed by scalding tears of sorrow for his betrayal of Jesus and he had been saved from despair by the purifying comfort of the Holy Spirit. Then, the blunt impetuosity of the Galilean fisherman was transformed into the patient wisdom of Christ's First Vicar on earth.

St. Paul did not become the great Apostle of the Gentiles until he had experienced agonizing sorrow for having persecuted the Lord of Glory. Jesus sent to the stricken persecutor a Christian named Ananias, who baptized the penitent, imparting to him the Holy Spirit. The mighty solace of God the Holy Spirit made of the man who had done much evil to Christ's saints in Jerusalem a vessel of election, to carry the name of Jesus before the Gentiles and kings and the children of Israel.

We know from the history of the Church how often those engaged in apostolic work have been tested by the sorrow of being misunderstood. St. Paul was misunderstood by the Apostles, and was called to Jerusalem to defend himself at the First Council. At the time of the Popes and anti-popes, there were saints on both sides. During twenty years, St. John of the Cross was misunderstood and ill-treated by his religious brethren. St. Alphonsus Liguori was expelled from the Redemptorist Order he had founded. All of these men grew in God's grace during adversity, because the Holy Spirit was their solace.

## Tests of Endurance

If these tremendous griefs occur in the lives of the saints, we must certainly expect the small sorrows and slight misunderstandings God fits to our weaker natures. Usually physical hardships do not depress us unduly. We soon learn, too, how to sympathize with our Christians in their grief, and yet not lose our own equilibrium of soul. This control of our emotions is a necessity for priests who have to attend funerals constantly. Our work in itself is not grievous, but we can suffer acutely because of personal misunderstandings that occur in the course of our labors.

Sometimes a mission superior is obliged to fill a sudden vacancy, and that may mean transferring two or three individuals. The plans of the priests in question are disrupted by the change, and they may feel that the superior has not given sufficient thought to their particular problems and projects. Perhaps they write letters of explanatory protest to the superior and the latter makes a matter-of-fact reply, saying that the changes are for the good of the work as a whole.

If the missioners concerned give way to touchy self-pity and brood over the personal calamities involved, they may even come to think of the superior as vindictive, whereas he was merely preoccupied with the needs of the whole mission field. On the other hand, if the men in question take their personal disappointments to God the Holy Spirit, His enlightening solace will make them fully satisfied to cooperate selflessly in the progress of the work as a whole.

We have to learn to see our petty griefs as tests of endurance. They ought to make us much more sympathetic to others in their trials. Above all, our little sufferings should make us think with a measure of understanding of the grief we cause God by sin.

## Surmounting Self-Pity

If unintentional acts of others hurt us so keenly, what can we say of our own intentional acts against God? Instead of giving way to sterile self-pity, we should seek the purifying help of the Holy Spirit in making sorrow for sin our greatest grief. This sorrow is fertile, because it lifts us from selfish preoccupations to healthy concern about our relations with God.

We ought to be sorry for even the smallest venial sin. Father Price used to say often to the pioneer Maryknoll students: "The least venial sin means that much less glory given to God, and that for all eternity." So, we ought to grieve for the irreparable loss caused by our fault. Sorrow for having offended God should be our greatest grief, but so often it is not.

Christian sorrow for sin is not despair or discouragement, because the Holy Spirit strengthens in our souls a sure knowledge of God's mercy. In one of the prayers of the Mass, we find the words: "O God, Whose property, nature, it is to be merciful and forgiving." Forgiveness is an inalienable part of God's love for us; and to be always aware of our need of God's mercy is the one safeguard against sin. We should experience a wonder that we have offended so loving and merciful a God, together with a healthy fear of our own weakness in the future. Like St. Philip Neri, who used to pray daily that he be kept that day from committing sin, we need a sane dread of sin.

## Sanctifying Sorrow

While a dread of sin insures that we will not make purely routine confessions, it does not mean that we should be afraid of seeking the Sacrament of Penance. Such a fear may be an indication that we do not appreciate the Sacrament as God's Mercy Seat. We are glorifying the infinite mercy of God by kneeling in His presence and confessing our sins, sure that He will receive us once again with open arms.

If we are tormented by scruples in our examination of conscience, we should depend the more on the solace of the Holy Spirit Who alone can enable us to resist the temptation of dreading confession. Every time we receive the Sacrament of Penance, God in His Mercy increases the indwelling of the Holy Spirit in our souls. The Third Person of the Blessed Trinity, solacing our scrupulous sufferings, will transform excessive preoccupation with self into sanctifying sorrow.

Do not receive the Sacrament of Penance with a routine dryness of soul. As in all other grievous weariness, the Holy Spirit is our solace in combating the lassitude of monotony. He will transform our weak, selfish staleness into an abiding and lively sorrow for sin. When this purifying sorrow informs our souls, it leaves no place of entry for the corroding pangs of self-pity.

## Eleven

# Come, Blessed Light

God made the sacramental universe in His image, and He has repeatedly manifested Himself to mankind under the appearance of light. In the story of creation in the Book of Genesis, we read: "The Spirit of God moved over the waters. And God said: Be light made. And light was made. And God saw the light that it was good" *(Gen. I: 2–4)*. In its shining and its warmth, the created light was a finite, material image of God's Spirit of Love.

God enlightened the souls of our first parents; and when they turned away from His Spirit of Love by willful disobedience, He did not abandon them and their descendants to outer darkness. In His infinite mercy, God willed that all men should be saved; and He prepared for the coming on earth of His Divine Son, "the Light of the World."

In the long centuries preceding the Incarnation, God chose the Jews as the people who should keep burning amid pagan darkness the light of faith in the True God. He prepared them for their great mission by appearing to Moses as a light, a flame in the burning bush. When God gave His Commandments and His Covenant to Moses on Mt. Sinai, the Jews in the valley below saw the summit of the mountain in flaming radiance.

God protected His chosen people from the surrounding darkness of pagan idolatry and its constant temptations. During the exodus from Egypt, He went before the Jews as a shining pillar of cloud by day and a pillar of fire by night. Again and again in the centuries that followed, God manifested His light to the Jews by pouring it forth into the souls of inspired prophets.

## Fire on the Earth

In the fullness of time, the Second Person of the Blessed Trinity became flesh for the salvation of the world. An aged and devout man in Jerusalem, named Simeon, had been told by the Holy Spirit that he would not die before he had seen the Christ of the Lord. The old man was in the temple when, according to the law of Moses, Mary and Joseph brought the Infant Jesus to present Him to God.

Simeon took the Child into his arms and blessed God, saying: "Now Thou dost dismiss Thy servant, O Lord, according to Thy word in peace. My eyes have seen Thy salvation, which Thou hast prepared before the face of all peoples: a light to the revelation of the Gentiles and the glory of Thy people Israel" *(Luke II: 28–32).*

The light of faith in the True God, kept burning amid pagan darkness by the people of Israel, now manifested itself with divine effulgence in the Infant Christ. Henceforth this light was not merely to be preserved; it had to be spread to all the Gentiles, to all the peoples of the earth still groping in darkness and the shadow of death. Our Lord would say to His disciples: "I have come to cast fire upon the earth, and what will I but that it be kindled?" *(Luke XII: 49)*

After Christ had instituted the Sacrament of the Holy Eucharist, He prayed to His Father in heaven for the disciples so soon to be stricken by His Crucifixion. The sublime prayer of Jesus for His followers was that they might all be one with the Blessed Trinity, as the light of the world; that the splendor of the Godhead might shine through them also, for the salvation of all humanity.

At Pentecost, Jesus sent to His disciples the fullness of divine light in God the Holy Spirit, Who appeared as tongues of fire, teaching all truth to those transfigured Christians. Hitherto downcast and fearful, they became consumed with zeal to spread the light that was in them, the divine fire of the knowledge and the love of God. The light of the Holy Spirit has been poured forth on baptized Christians ever since that first Pentecost; and they are not true followers of Jesus, the Light of the World, who do not long and strive to spread the divine radiance.

## Freely Have We Received

God gives us free will, so He desires that the Christian should use that will to love Him and to choose Him before all else. When we have voluntarily chosen God as our portion, then He floods us with light; He goes before us to keep our unsure feet from stumbling.

We do not have to struggle to discover the truth, as would a pagan. God has guaranteed the infallibility of the Church. He has given us an ark of the new covenant, in the custody of the successors of St. Peter; and He has promised that this ark will never be in darkness. God has given us the same light that guided all the saints who have walked in it before us. What they have done we, also, can will to accomplish.

In the Sacrament of Baptism, God fills each Christian personally with light; and He strengthens the illumination of the Christian soul in the Sacrament of Confirmation. He has given us as guides on our way the Holy Scriptures and the writings of inspired Christians, infallibly interpreted by His Church. To the Angelic Doctor, St. Thomas Aquinas, Our Lord said, "Thomas, thou has written well of Me." With these and other innumerable daily promptings, God the Holy Spirit compasses us about with light, so that we may not stray into darkness and follow will-o'-the-wisps.

God has filled our souls with a light so brilliant and all powerful that sometimes we cannot even see it; and we are not conscious of it very often. It would be well for us, then, to stand for a few moments in front of this light, fully conscious of its divine radiance, and asking ourselves why God has chosen to grant it to us personally from our baptism. Theologians tell us that if there had been only one man on earth, God the Son would have become incarnate and suffered His Passion to save that one soul. But there are still many men on earth ignorant of the Lord of Glory. As followers of Christ and bearers of the light, what is our responsibility toward them?

## Freely Should We Give

Christ did not send God the Holy Spirit to His first followers in order that they might merely keep the fullness of the divine light in their own hearts. He told His disciples, "So let your light shine before men that they may see your good works and glorify your Father Who is in heaven" *(Matt. V: 16)*.

How can we truly love Christ, the Light of the World, and not be aflame with the desire to serve as lightbearers to those who still do not believe in the Redemption? The Apostle St. Paul was so driven by zeal to enlighten the blindness of the Jews that he wished to suffer even an anathema, or curse, for the sake of their stubborn souls.

It was St. Paul, also, who said that apostles are the glory of Christ. Our Lord gives special lights to the apostolic Christian, and He goes on before him in all his journeyings after souls. The lightbearer's own heart is lightsome and burns within him for joy, as he speaks with his Master on the way to the salvation of the nations.

Come, Holy Spirit, Blessed Light, and fill the hearts of Thy faithful. Flood the depths of our souls with Thy radiance and grace and strength, so that we, too, may be to unbelievers a shining and a burning light.

## Twelve

# Keep Us United to the Blessed Trinity

Apart from God, we are nothing; and everything is harmful to us. That is a wonderful way of summing up the relation between God and ourselves. He is the light and the life of the universe; we are nothing. This is strikingly evident in those very domains from which modern materialists have striven hardest to exclude God.

Modern technical inventions, for instance, are very clear examples of light from God. Most inventors, after they have become famous and rich, are not afraid to be sincere. They admit that after a long period of study and experimentation, they often seemed to make their discoveries as if by accident; they hit upon the right scheme. The world is simply full of all sorts of ingenious devices, especially in this mechanical age, that are really lights from God the Holy Spirit.

The whole world is dependent on God. The food we eat, the crops, the rotation and prodigalities of nature—all manifest the Providence of God. "Can a woman forget her infant, so as not to have pity on the son of her womb? And if she should forget, yet will I not forget you," says the Lord to His human creatures *(Isai. XLIX: 15)*. His light shines on the just and on the wicked; it shines on the whole world. Even in the hearts of pagans there is implanted some sort of recognition of this truth, which affords the Christian apostle a starting point for revealing to them a knowledge of the True God. They see the reasonableness of the existence of a Universal Providence, which is in itself another light from the Holy Spirit.

## The New Heresy

In his book called *Survivals and New Arrivals,* Hilaire Belloc discusses the nature of heresies, past and present. He says that the heresy of the present age is totally unlike all past heretical aberrations. In the past, men took some one truth, and by emphasizing it at the expense of all the others, got it out of focus. They ended in error; but they had started with some truth, some light of the Holy Spirit.

This is apparent in Protestant heresies. Founders of Protestant sects stressed so strongly the role of faith in the salvation of souls that they ended by casting out works. They concentrated their attention upon the light of the Holy Spirit revealed in the Sacred Scriptures, and then decided to take it as their sole guide. They wanted no intermediaries between themselves and God, so they denied the need of the priesthood. In brief, they fixed their whole attention on one truth, one light of the Holy Spirit, and then distorted it.

Even the pagan philosophers of antiquity based their systems on some fundamental light given by God to the natural reason of men of good will. Thus, Pliny the Elder wrote: "It is ridiculous to suppose that the great head of all things, whatever it be, pays any regard to human affairs." Pliny recognized the truth of the existence of a "great head of all things"; but natural reason alone could not reveal to him the divine mystery of God's love for every human creature.

Confucius started from an appreciation of the truth and beauty of virtue; but his natural reason did not show him supernatural motives for attaining it. Buddha perceived that all men strive after happiness; but he could not know how God uses this supernaturalized yearning to draw Christian hearts to Himself. Consequently, Buddha fell into the error of teaching that happiness consists in nirvana, the absence of desire.

But the new paganism, the new heresy, does not even start out with a fundamental truth. It is a departure from the past, in the sense that its very foundation is an untruth. It begins to build on the false premise that man is sufficient unto himself, that he can do anything. So the perverted neopaganism of our age has spawned Nietzsche's superman, Hitler's super-race, and the Soviets' deification of collective man. The new paganism has turned away from fundamental truths evident to thinkers throughout the ages and is concerned only with happiness in this world.

## A Subjective Sanction

Even Catholics have been affected to some extent by this modern heresy, because it is all around us. We see people following a creed that is more and more based on the supremacy of man, a religion that seeks no sanction for things beyond the feeling that they are necessary for individual happiness. In our public schools, little mention is made of the Godhead; and the emphasis is on preparing for success in this world, rather than on adherence to sound Christian principles.

Before World War I, people of our Western civilization as a whole respected the Bible and Christian ethics. They made a reasoned effort to live up to the Christian code; and if they failed, they did not consider themselves justified because their emotions had got the better of them. But one of the effects of World War I was a loosening of the passions, the emotions. This giving way to the emotions was followed by acceptance of their subjective sanction of what is true and good.

In Catholic circles, there began to be much less emphasis on penance and mortification. Services were shortened, and many sought to be excused from the Lenten fast. The Church takes into consideration the fact that we have been weakened by our environment and fits the burden to our backs. But many of us have gone further than the prudent concessions of Mother Church. We have yielded to a constant tendency to evade rules and to liberate whims.

Bishop James A. Walsh, the Co-Founder of our Maryknoll Society, said to me on numerous occasions that he was puzzled by the excuses people gave for failing in their duties. Catholics, as well as others, are apt to say, "Well, I do not like to do that particular thing." Now, Catholics before World War I would never have made such an excuse, because they would have realized at once its complete invalidity.

Likes and dislikes have very little to do with our duty. To take our individual emotions as a criterion of truth is a tacit recognition that each man is sufficient unto himself. A very strong proof that we Catholics have been affected by this modem heresy is the fact that so many of us do not prize humility. It appears to us as something exterior, superfluous, and bothersome. In fact, it sometimes seems to me that the next generation won't even know what the word "humility" means.

## Abysses of Nothingness

Father Price used to tell the pioneer Maryknollers that, apart from God, we human beings are abysses of nothingness. We tried hard to be convinced of this and so to acquire real humility. But the apostle, like all other mortals, is not immune to pride. Complacency is always ready to sneak in, as the missioner thinks of *his* successful catechumenate or the mounting number of *his* converts. If we are impatient with ourselves or with others, or if we only grudgingly admit the superiority of others, it is a sure sign of lack of humility.

Perhaps it might be objected, after all, that if a person has thought out a plan and it proves extraordinarily successful, he cannot help a certain feeling of complacency. Well, the remedy for this natural self-satisfaction is to remind ourselves anew that all our powers and all our talents are from God. St. Paul tells us that both the power to will and power to do are given to us by God, the Father of light. About all we have done is, more than once, to get in the way.

## He Is Our Safeguard

Not only is man nothing without God; but apart from God, all things are harmful to him. If we love anyone apart from God, we become a prey to tormenting passion. The moment we put a value on anything and do not take God into account, we are moving toward spiritual ruin. Without God, there is nothing in us that is not hurtful to our own souls.

True humility, then, is not only the recognition that we ourselves are nothing without God but the realization that the whole universe subsists only in Him. It is the fact that God informs the whole sacramental universe that makes it of any value. When we seek to exclude God from the world and from ourselves, we have rejected the essence of Life and are vainly seeking nourishment for our souls from harmful abysses of nothingness.

Let us, then, keep always before our minds and hearts the basic truth that in God we live, and move, and have our being. We do not need to beat our breasts and to keep harping on our nothingness in order to practice true humility. Real humility is more than skin-deep. It consists in a sincere conviction that all other people and the whole universe are sacred and holy, because of God's presence in them, and that everything we ourselves have is loaned to us by the Blessed Trinity. Such is the attitude that will safeguard us in the new paganism which glorifies man as self-sufficient and has forgotten God. Now, as it was long ago in King David's day, only the fool says in his heart: "There is no God" *(Psalm XIII: 1)*.

## Thirteen

# Come, Purifier of Our Souls

In most social gatherings of today, it would be considered decidedly bad form to speak at length of God. Another topic sedulously avoided by the modern mind is sin. Yet Catholic theology teaches us that sin is the only real evil in the world; and it will not be eliminated by passing it over in silence.

Now, I do not mean to say that consideration of our own sins should make us sad. Sorrow for sin is healing, but sadness is unhealthy. The Church never intended that the Sacrament of Penance should make us sad. We call the Blessed Virgin Our Lady of Sorrows; but we do not think of her as being sad. Our Lord wept, but He was not sad; because sadness is a morose state, an over-indulgence in the emotional side of sorrow. The sorrow that the Church wants us to have for sin is a sorrow of the will, of the understanding. Our grief should not be primarily for selfish reasons, but because sin offends

God. The horror of sin is that it turns away from the Light of the World.

## By His Bruises We Are Healed

In His infinite love for fallen mankind, God the Son became incarnate, took upon Himself the burden of our sins, and merited for us forgiveness. Isaiah foretold the Passion of Christ in the sublime passage: "He was wounded for our iniquities; He was bruised for our sins. The chastisement of our peace was upon Him; and by His bruises we are healed" *(Isai. LIII: 5)*.

What is more, Christ is always living to make intercession for us. In heaven, He shows His Father the wounds that He suffered for our salvation. With divine yearning for the souls redeemed by the Precious Blood, God the Father and God the Son send down to dwell in us their cleansing Spirit of Love, God the Holy Spirit.

Is there, then, any reason why we should let sin overcome us by sadness? We insult God afresh when we are discouraged by sin, because we thereby confess that we dare not hope in the Passion of Our Savior and in the purifying power of God the Holy Spirit. When St. Paul asked the Lord to deliver him from a certain weakness, God answered, "My grace is sufficient for thee, for power is made perfect in infirmity." Then the Apostle rejoiced, saying, "Gladly therefore will I glory in my infirmities that the power of Christ may dwell in me" *(II Cor. XII: 9)*.

We, also, casting out sadness, can glory in our infirmities. By so doing, we adore God, we make an act of confidence in Him. We prove that we truly recognize our utter dependence on Him, that we are certain the grace won for us by the Passion of Christ is sufficient for the remission of our sins. We rejoice in Our Lord, Who came to give life and to give it more abundantly. We render thanks for the lights given us through the indwelling in our souls of God the Holy Spirit, the Divine Purifier.

### *The Bridge of San Luis Rey*

While we should strive to become holy enough to glory in our infirmities, in the Spirit of St. Paul, we cannot for a moment afford to forget the true nature of evil. Affected by the materialistic thinking of our age, we tend to consider poverty and physical ugliness as evils in themselves. These things have no essential connection whatever with sin, and only sin is evil. The Sinless Christ chose poverty as His earthly portion, and more than once He has appeared to his saints in the hideous guise of a leper.

In our times war has come to be regarded as such an unmitigated evil that sinful concessions have been made for the sake of peace. Yet, war can bring out heroic virtues in men. We have only to recall St. Joan of Arc to realize that the warrior can be a great servant of God. War is not the evil, but rather the sinful passions that provoke the conflict.

I recall a striking book by Thornton Wilder, *The Bridge of San Luis Rey*. Wilder relates to us the life history of the different people who were crossing this bridge when it collapsed. The new paganism would count this accident a tragic calamity, and even Catholics might unthinkingly view it as such. But the author makes us see that for each of the persons then crossing the bridge, its collapse was a mercy of God in disguise, taking them away from sin, the only evil.

To see where real evil lies, we must strive to look at things from God's viewpoint. In the light of His spotless purity, sin is revealed in all its horrible evil. Come, pure light of the Holy Spirit, so that we may see clearly where the evil of sin lurks.

## A Spirit of Expiation

Our sorrow for sin, for having turned away from God Our Creator, should include the motive of expiation. After the great grace that we receive in the Sacrament of Penance, our sins are washed away; but we still have the same tendencies to yield to sin again, and the same temptations surround us in the daily circumstances of our life. We have to take precautionary measures against these imminent dangers to cleanness of soul, because only the pure of heart shall see God.

Our attitude toward these dangers is all important. We must consider any likelihood of soiling our souls by sin as the greatest potential evil that threatens us. The fervent Christian should not recoil only before mortal sin; the smallest venial sin stains our souls. We are called to perfection, so we can't make fine distinctions or quibble about the measure in which we risk to offend God. It is hard not to have pity on ourselves in regard to minor failings, especially omissions. But anything that will give less glory to God is a sin, the only abhorrent evil in creation. Everything else in the world obeys and serves God; only we, by an abuse of the free will He gave us, sin by turning away from His light.

So, in considering sin we have to strive after the divine viewpoint that dwells with satisfaction only on spotlessness. We must ask God the Holy Spirit, the Purifier, to wash from our souls the stains that remain after sin is forgiven, the inclinations to renewed evil. If we think of our sins and weaknesses in a spirit of expiation, the load of sadness is lifted. Our effort to make amends becomes united with the Divine Sacrifice on the Cross at the Mass. Our life becomes a unit with the Passion of Christ. We aspire with strong and humble hope to the company of the saints washed pure in the Blood of the Lamb of God.

If we have offended some human being who loves us and have begged pardon and been forgiven, we are careful not to repeat the same fault and we try to make amends by extra acts of thoughtfulness. Such must be our spirit of expiation for having sinned against God, Who loves us with an eternal love. He has gladly forgiven us; and we should show our joy in His forgiveness by seeking extra means of pleasing Him, as a proof of our abiding desire of amendment. The abiding sorrow for sin that we read about in theology books and in the writings of the Christian mystics, must become a cleansing reality in our own lives. It is the only sure safeguard against the soiling sordidness of renewed sin.

## Love Founded on Humility

Our spirit of expiation in considering sin should be not so much a memory of particular acts in the past by which we have turned from God, but rather a horror of the sordidness of sin in any form. We should have a horror of serving idols, whether our idolatry consists in placing ourselves first, or in serving other human beings apart from God.

So we ask God the Holy Spirit to purify us anew. He washes us in Baptism, and He cleanses us in the Sacrament of Penance. Now we beg Him to keep us spotless, seeing clearly our utter dependence on Him and our own weakness. This prayer to God the Holy Spirit is just as much an act of love as one more formally expressed. Perhaps it is more truly an act of love, because it is loving trust founded on humility.

Come, Holy Spirit, Purifier of our souls. Give us the light to see sin always for what it really is, in all its loathsome evil; and grant us the grace to look with ever increasing yearning on the beauty of holiness.

## Fourteen

# Give Us the Dew of Heaven

From the viewpoint of God, our work for Him is intended to lead us to our own salvation. So it is well for us to try to view our work as a whole and apart from our own emotions. We shall not succeed entirely in this effort, of course. As human beings, we are naturally so subjective that if we see a picture of a sailboat, we mentally put ourselves in the boat and admire ourselves in those enviable circumstances more than the picture itself.

Nevertheless, we should try very hard to acquire pure, impersonal motives in our work, because we can become just as narrow-minded and selfish, as priests and missioners, as in any other walk of life. Theoretically, our vocation is to labor to lead the souls of all mankind to God. Our work ought to have the breadth and scope of the Universal Church and should therefore breed in us a world-wide heart. But I think it is the common experience of apostles that we tend to become very localized, very set on one particular place. Instead of trying to view our parish or mission as a tiny unit in God's sublime design for the salvation of souls, we are more likely to consider it a central vantage point from which we see only what affects our narrow little corner.

During my first year in China, I began unconsciously to be unduly impressed with my personal share in the Church's apostolate. Probably God allowed me this distorted view as a consolation to my weakness in strange work in a far land. But Father Price, Maryknoll's Co-Founder and first Mission Superior, wished to make sure that I should advance to a higher viewpoint and purer motives. He rebuked me gently, saying, "Even in the articles that you write for *The Field Afar,* you always refer to *my* work, *my* mission, even *my* Chinese." I had not realized this until Father Price pointed it out; but what he said was perfectly true.

## Away with Self-Pity

It is not so bad when a young parish priest or missioner brags a bit about his own work, while comparing it with that of others. We can see the humorous side of his self-importance, and we are indulgent with an enthusiasm untempered by experience. The complainers and the whiners are the people who are hard to stand. But the fact is, that the self-important apostle who fails to keep his eyes on God's design as a whole and thus to acquire purer motives becomes a prime target for self-pity when disillusionment sets in. Aridity parches his soul and he sees his field of labor as a barren desert.

We are warned in the seminary that the apostolate is a daily crucifixion; but we look on the warning merely as a magnificent challenge to our zeal for God and souls. Then we arrive on the mission field, and we discover what monotonous, humdrum agony it can be to carry our cross for only a few hours. If we cannot lift our eyes from our own little trials and strivings to the splendor of God's salvation of mankind, self-pity soon shrivels our souls. If we find ourselves thinking that our efforts are always misunderstood, we could recall with profit that St. John of the Cross was kept in prison by his own religious brethren during a quarter of a century. He was accused of heresy, because he was endeavoring to reform his order, and at one period he was nearly burned at the stake. How many of us have been misunderstood by our confreres, to the point of persecution almost unto death?

When we bemoan the sterility of our mission field, we might think of the missioners who work among the Moslems of northern Africa. They are allowed into the region on the sole condition that they do not teach Christianity. Their bishop forbids them to baptize anyone, because if they received only one or two Moslems into the Catholic Church, there would be danger of a fierce persecution accompanied by expulsion. Those missioners in northern Africa really have it hard. If they stopped for self-pity, not one of them would be able to persevere.

Have we ever at any time suffered from spiritual aridity to the same agonizing extent as did St. Teresa of Avila? Are the difficulties of our mission field in any way to be compared with the long solitude endured by Charles de Foucauld among the Tuaregs of the Sahara Desert? We must not be too ready, then, to see ourselves as handicapped martyrs, pursued by failures and constant misrepresentations. Psychologists say that when we are confronted with hard, unpleasant work with an element of possible failure in it, we instinctively build up what is called a defense complex. We hurriedly seek an alibi in our unsuccessful work; we want to shift the blame.

## Beyond Human Measure

How can any of us really judge what work for God is a success, and what a failure? Can we form a just estimate of where praise or blame is merited? As Ordinary of the Hakka mission field, I never take it on myself to praise any of the Fathers for the work they are doing. If they are working solely for God, my praise is superfluous and of small account. If they are trying to please me, they are working from a wrong motive; and no praise is due.

Human measures of success and failure mean nothing in our work for souls. If you remember, one of the reasons King David displeased God was because he tried to make an estimate of his own work. It is a temptation for all of us. We compare our apostolate with that of a confrere and we find reasons for estimating that, on the whole, our success has been the more outstanding one. Such attempts to take the measure of our own work are in themselves failures and can unbalance our spiritual outlook.

Our work is barren, or is a success, only if God considers it as such. So, it is worse than useless to worry about what we ourselves or other human beings may think of it. After all, it is not our work, but simply the work we are at present doing for God. We have merely to give Him unstinted service, confident that He is never outdone in generosity. For the rest, neither we nor our superiors can measure how God estimates our work, until Judgment Day.

## Have Confidence

Our Divine Master tells us, "Have confidence, I have overcome the world" *(John XVI: 33)*. By what men considered as the failure of His Cross, Our Lord triumphed over all the estimates of worldly wisdom. We must follow, then, with absolute trust where He leads us, even when human beings despise us as the most abject of men.

Confidence in God does not mean that it is wrong to ask Him for strengthening consolation. He wants us to turn to Him in our difficulties and our dryness of spirit. "Ask, and it shall be given you, seek, and you shall find," Our Lord promised those who trust in Him *(Matt. VII: 7).*

At the same time, however, we must be prepared to plod along, even if the going continues to be against the grain. God Himself may be sending us this aridity in prayer and in our work, in order that our motives may be purified. The peace that passes all human understanding cannot be measured by the yardstick of the natural emotions. St. Paul tells us that God the Father willed that heaven's peace should come through the Cross of the Son of His love *(Col. I: 20).*

So, whether we are working in the Far East or in the Sahara Desert, among Negroes in the State of South Carolina or among the elite on Fifth Avenue, New York City, it is all God's work and it will be measured solely from His viewpoint. Justice and mercy are in His keeping; and work which appears easier to us is often accompanied by greater obligations. Come, Holy Spirit, Giver of the dew of heaven. Water with Thy graces the aridity of our souls and of our labors, and our wilderness shall become a garden of God. "Joy and gladness shall be found therein, thanksgiving and the voice of praise" *(Isai. LI: 3).*

## Fifteen

# Make Holy Our Broken Hearts

All of us suffer from agonizing intimate distresses that are not primarily the wounds inflicted by personal sin or by difficult exterior circumstances. These distresses are the end result of heredity, upbringing, and everything that has contributed to the molding of our individual natures. They are rooted in the subconscious; and we need the light of the Holy Spirit to enable us to acquire a sane view of them.

When we take our deep interior trials to another human being, molded by different influences, he cannot give us truly understanding healing. The trials that loom before us as mountains, he sees as mere molehills. We are oversensitive, he thinks; and in his misplaced kindness, he may unman us by the wrong kind of sympathy. Then we are less able to cope sanely with our distresses of the soul than we were before we had recourse to this human comfort.

## In God's Arms

Now it is true that apostles are among the most sensitive of men. If they had not been keenly sensitive to the yearning love of God for souls still in darkness and the shadow of death, if they had not been powerfully moved by the destitution of these pagan souls, they would never have been attracted to their vocation in the first place. Apostles are followers of Christ Our Lord, Whose Sacred Heart overflowed with sensitive compassion for the multitudes. We are sensitive; and we have to learn to imitate our Divine Master in seeking comfort only in the Blessed Trinity. When we seek healing elsewhere for the deep wounds of our soul, it is but to our harm.

This is the theme of the profoundly Catholic poem The Hound of Heaven, by Francis Thompson. He shows us a soul that in its sensitive human weakness dreads to yield entirely to God's tremendous love, "lest, having Him, it must have naught beside." Everything spurns and hurts this wounded soul, until at last it turns without reserve to God and hears Him say:

> "All which I took from thee I did but take,
> Not for thy harms,
> But just that thou might'st seek it in My arms.
> All which thy child's mistake
> Fancies as lost, I have stored for thee at home:
> Rise, clasp My hand, and come!"

## The Apostolic Dilemma

Not only must the apostle seek comfort solely in God, but he must train the souls in his care to do likewise. He may not show them the wrong kind of sympathy. When I was consecrated Bishop of my missionary diocese, I chose as my motto, "*Condolere*," to suffer, to sympathize with others. The Scriptures tell us the high priest knows his own weakness. He knows it, indeed, and it inclines him strongly to help others in their interior trials; but in his compassion he has to be careful not to stand in God's way. This must be one of the Holy Father's greatest hardships. He is keenly aware of his own weakness; but as Vicar of Christ, he dare not show a softening sympathy to others.

Years ago my elder brother, a businessman, taught me a lesson I have never forgotten. Shortly after I had entered the Maryknoll seminary, my mother died and I was called home. My brother met me at the door and said, "Now Frank, there is not going to be any crying around here; because it would unsettle Father, unman him." My brother's putting it that way gave us all strength to bear our grief by turning for comfort to God alone.

The apostle's special dilemma, then, is to know to what degree he can afford to sympathize with others, without standing in God's way and thereby weakening both himself and those he seeks to comfort. He must sometimes remain aloof, even at the risk of misunderstanding. He is set to train souls to seek God, and God only. If he allows his converts to depend unduly on his human sympathy, he misleads them and diminishes his own spiritual strength.

We all love to be appreciated; and it is so easy to make life very pleasant for others and for ourselves by being soft. When we are tempted in this way, it will help us to think of Our Lord in the Garden of Olives. Christ's agony was unto death, so that His sweat became as drops of blood, trickling down upon the ground. God the Father sent an angel to His Beloved Son, not to take away the Savior's distress; but to strengthen Him.

Again, we can fight against our tendency to softness by imagining ourselves on Calvary. Christ hanging on His Cross looks down on His Mother, and He knows that there is no sorrow like unto her sorrow. He is her son, but He is also her God; so He does not speak words of human consolation. Instead, He associates His Mother afresh in the redemption of mankind by naming her the Mother of St. John, our representative as children of Mary. The Blessed Virgin receives the divine consolation of sharing in a unique manner in Her Son's Passion. She does not give way to personal grief; she *stands* at the foot of the Cross.

## The Crown of Thorns

While I was in the United States on a decennial visit, I attended a ceremony for the reception of novices at the Motherhouse of the Maryknoll Sisters. The presiding priest offered each postulant about to receive the habit the choice of a crown of roses or a crown of thorns; and the young women chose the crown of thorns. This is a beautiful symbol of the attitude God wants his apostles to take in their work for souls. God the Holy Spirit inspires them to choose suffering with Christ, without turning to human consolation in their mental distresses. When some interior suffering disturbs me overmuch, I often think of St. Noel Chabanel, a Jesuit missioner who worked among the Huron Indians in Canada in the seventeenth century. Father Chabanel had been a brilliant professor in the Jesuit colleges of France; but when he arrived in Canada, he discovered that he was incapable of mastering the Indian tongues. He was never able in Huronia to do more than baptize and say Mass. Moreover, humanly speaking, he loathed the savages, their food, their grossness, and their filth.

Father Chabanel could have sought to lay aside this terrible crown of thorns by seeking the sympathetic understanding of his superiors. Instead, he made a vow never to ask to return to France. He endured this living martyrdom among the Hurons for long years before his turn came to shed his blood for the Faith. And we can be sure that in the midst of his interior anguish, the Jesuit apostle knew the peace and joy of glorying in His Master's Crown of Thorns.

God who made us knows our weakness; and to most of us He does not send interior trials so great as those endured by St. Noel Chabanel. But we all have our personal sorrows, and only God can understand how grievous they appear from our limited viewpoint. Come, Holy Spirit, we know Thy power to make sane and holy our broken hearts. Unlike human comforters, Thou canst console us without taking away our crown of thorns and the cross that weighs us down.

The Holy Spirit gives us the light and the strength to impersonalize our anguish and rejoice in the middle of our pain that God has entrusted to us a share in the evolving Passion of the Mystical Body of Christ. "When thou shalt arrive thus far, that tribulation becomes sweet and savory to thee for the love of Christ, then think that it is well with thee, for thou hast found a paradise upon earth," wrote the author of *The Imitation*.

## Sixteen

# Incline Our Wills to Obey

One of the invocations in the Sequence for Pentecost asks God the Holy Spirit to bend what is rigid. People outside of the Church tend to look on her laws as extremely rigid. As for members of a religious order or society who take a vow of obedience, non-Catholics find it hard to believe that such individuals do not become hidebound automatons. And we ourselves sometimes find it painfully difficult to bend our rigidly selfish wills to glad obedience. It is then that we must ask God the Holy Spirit to make the commandments and the regulations of the Church come alive to us, so that we may understand that they are the voice of Christ.

Any doctor can take a bundle of bones and make a skeleton of it; but only God can clothe the skeleton with flesh and blood and make it the framework of a living body. To make law applicable in all cases is beyond human powers, so that in reality, the rigidity lies in the law codes of the various nations, whereas the laws of the Church pulsate with the life of the Mystical Body of Christ.

### Where Blind Obedience Really Lies

"Liberals" castigate the obedience of Catholics to Church law as being blind. The truth is that it is the other shoe that pinches. In the first place, the law codes of the various nations contain so many constantly increasing regulations that even a lawyer would find it difficult to keep abreast of them. Yet ignorance of the secular law is no excuse. How can it be said that the obedience thus exacted to an unknown law is enlightened?

After World War I, President Wilson called on the Holy Father, and he gave the Vatican Library a huge set of richly bound law volumes. I think there were something like sixteen hundred immense volumes in the set. Then the Pope presented President Wilson, in return, with one small volume of Canon Law; and Benedict XV told his distinguished guest that the little volume regulated the lives of all the hundreds of millions of Catholics in the world. It is marvelous how the Church had codified all our needs, our desires, and our actions, in laws that are eternally true and made accessible to all the faithful. Even in matters of etiquette, the rules of the Church make sense, while the regulations of worldly etiquette, though often incomprehensible, exact blind obedience. When Catholics use the titles of "Reverend" Father and "Reverend" Sister, they really mean that the persons thus addressed are to be revered. But in the language of worldly etiquette, we use the address "Dear Sir" in writing to a person utterly unknown to us. Of course we do not mean that term of affection, any more than we mean the decreed manner of closing the letter, the "ever truly yours." This worldly etiquette, to which society expects us to give unreasoning obedience, is a skeleton rattling dead, rigid formulae. The Church, on the other hand, has kept its etiquette alive with true meaning.

## Obedience Makes Us One with Christ

Far from exacting blind obedience on the part of her members, the Church teaches that obedience has value only when it is given with open eyes. Itis true that the Church requires a vow of obedience from those who consecrate themselves in a special way to the service of God; but she demands that this vow be freely made, with a full understanding of its obligations.

At my episcopal consecration, the Church did not permit just one general vow of obedience. I had to make about twenty-five particular vows of obedience. They asked me if I would obey Canon Law, and I vowed to do so. Then they requested a vow of obedience to the rules and regulations of the Church, another vow of obedience to the rules and regulations of the Councils . . . and so on, until I had made some twenty-five vows. The Church wanted to be sure that there was no blindness at all in the obedience the new bishop was vowing.

The vow of obedience, as it is made by those specially consecrated to God's service in the Catholic Church, is the most rationally noble act of which a human being is capable. He acknowledges by this vow that everything he has belongs to God; and he promises that he will use these gifts of God accordingly as the Divine Giver tells him. He offers to God all that he, in turn, has to give—his free will. Throughout the Christian centuries Catholics have given obedience to the Pope, the Vicar of Christ on earth. This obedience has made the Catholic Church the most powerful religious unit in the world. Because of the unbroken apostolic succession in the True Church, the obedience that unifies the Mystical Body of Christ takes us back to the Chair of Peter. To St. Peter, His first Vicar on earth, Our Lord said: "Whatsoever thou shalt bind upon earth, it shall be bound also in heaven" *(Matt. XVI: 19)*. Obedience is the point of unity that makes us one with Christ; and He was obedient even unto death.

## The Voice of Christ

Obedience weighs more heavily upon some natures than upon others. We are prone to criticize regulations and to discover excuses for our unwillingness to comply with them. Perhaps we want some big test of obedience, and we become very irritated with what we consider as niggling affronts to our own common sense.

This attitude reminds me of the pagan general in Syria who was afflicted with leprosy, and who heard of the miracles of healing of the Prophet Eliseus. He went down to Galilee with his army and sent one of his officers to the prophet to tell the wonder-worker that he had come to be cured. Eliseus was an old man and without stirring out of the house, he simply said, "Tell the general to wash seven times in the Jordan."

When the officer had repeated the words of the prophet to his general, the proud man was offended by the seemingly absurd simplicity of the order. "Are not the waters of Syria just as good as those of the Jordan River?" he asked angrily and started back to his own country. But the officer who had spoken with Eliseus said to the general: "If he had told you to accomplish some great act, you would have done it. Why not, then, this simple thing?" The general thought it over, went back to wash in the Jordan, and was cured by virtue of his obedience *(IV Kings V: 1–14)*.

We may also find that our pride recoils from an order that is put to us in a crude way. What could be cruder than the way in which human beings ordered their Savior to submit Himself to the ignominy of crucifixion? Christ humbled Himself and became obedient even unto the death of the Cross, because He recognized their hoarse shouts of "Crucify Him, Crucify Him" as instruments of His Divine Father's Will.

We cannot imitate Our Lord in His total obedience, unless we ask God the Holy Spirit to enable us to hear in the Church's laws the voice of Christ speaking to us. These laws are all regulations that were taught to St. Peter in germ by Our Lord Himself. They are acts of His Will, extending through the nerves of the Church, His Mystical Body. As members of this living Body, we breathe the Spirit of Christ when we obey its laws.

Come, Holy Spirit, and bend our wills to glad conformity to God's laws. By this obedience, the Truth of God's Commandments will set us free forever from the words that are the death of the soul—the terrible "I will not serve."

## Seventeen

# Come,
# Thou Fire of Love

Our means of familiar intercourse with God is prayer. We do not speak in terms of cold formality to human friends in whom we have put our trust; but we are conscious at times of a strange aloofness in our manner of conversing with God, our only Changeless Friend. We need the Holy Spirit, the Fire of Love, to burn away frozen places in our selfish hearts.

This point can bear emphasizing, especially in these days when the tendency is toward self reliance, reticence, and an implicit reluctance to prayer of petition. The growing attitude outside the Church might be summed up as: "What is the need of prayer? God knows what we need without our telling Him so."

## Holding Back from God's Friendship

Even among Catholics, there is a current feeling that begging God for material needs is less perfect and manly than other forms of prayer. Probably a subtle form of pride motivates our self-reliance. In human friendship we are often unwilling to ask a favor, though we know it would give pleasure to a friend to grant it. In like manner, we dislike putting ourselves under obligation even to God!

Can we discover the slightest justification for this attitude? We need not be afraid of incommoding God by our requests, because His resources are limitless. We are not in danger of selfishness when we ask God for favors, because we know that He will grant us only what is good for our soul. Finally, we need not feel that petition for spiritual and temporal necessities somehow implies lack of confidence in God's bounty, because He has expressly told us the contrary. Our Lord said to His Apostles: "All things whatsoever you ask when you pray, believe that you shall receive: and they shall come unto you" *(Mark XI: 24)*.

## The Little Way

Not only does friendship not count the cost, but it works both ways. It gives, and it also takes. We have to look on prayer of petition from God's point of view, rather than from the petty viewpoint of self-esteem. God is actually seeking means of helping us; but He wants us to ask for His favors, in order that we may grow in the strength and the warmth of our friendship for Him. He wishes us to become more conscious of the part He plays in our happiness. "Every best gift and every perfect gift is from above, coming down from the Father of lights, with Whom there is no change nor shadow of alteration," wrote St. James the Apostle *(James I: 17)*.

Perhaps we do not petition God often enough for our daily needs. It would not hurt us to be specific in asking His aid. God likes to work miracles of grace in our souls, and our childlike manner of trusting Him will win us favors. Such prayers for our daily needs are also little acts of humility, putting us in the position of beggars; and that is good for our souls. We can easily become stiff-necked even in our prayers, and such cold, formal worship of God is apt to be mere lip-service. But a prayer for something we need, something personal, something immediately useful, is apt to come warmly from the heart.

To speak to God with perfect trust in His changeless concern for our smallest needs is "the little way" shown us by St. Therese of Lisieux. Our Lord warned us, "Unless you be converted and become as little children, you shall not enter into the kingdom of heaven" *(Matt. XVIII: 3)*. So well founded are all the devotions encouraged by the Church that we cannot despise even the simplest of them without incurring danger of heresy. In like manner, the simple, childlike prayer of petition for petty needs implies a confession of faith in God's Omnipotence and Providence and takes on the grandeur of the entire liturgy.

## The Worth of the Individual Soul

One purpose of the Incarnation was to demonstrate to us the worth of the individual, the value in God's eyes of each and every soul of man. Because no one of us is too insignificant to be included in the eternal vision of God's plan, our petty needs are implicitly provided for; and none of our necessities is too small for God to stoop to. So we have no reason to feel uncomfortable in asking for simple things from God. He measures things by the pleasure they afford Him in giving them to us; by the trust we show in asking for them; and by the closer bonds they forge between Him and us. Anything that comes from God is sacramental and so cannot be of little account.

The prayer of petition, then, is especially useful in cultivating frequent intercourse with God, bringing Him into the petty details of our human lives. It reminds us constantly in many small ways that we are wholly dependent upon God, that He is always with us, and that we are rich in our credit with Him. The prayer of petition begets less worried concern for the future, less doubt of obtaining the means to accomplish our work, less mental fog when confronted with our own weakness, and less reliance on human aid.

We have so much to ask for. How often we fall into small faults that have become second nature to us, simply because we have not asked God's help in avoiding them. It will strengthen us enormously to be specific in asking God's grace for particular virtues, practical virtues that we can exercise here and now. If we need light on present problems, or if we are called on to make quick decisions, a turning to God in trust will relieve the situation. In work for souls, God may grant us a conversion if we ask it of Him with particular, confident insistence. By being specific in our request, we win God's added interest in the case. Incidentally, our fervent prayers increase our own efforts on behalf of the longed-for soul.

## The Saints Are Bold in Asking

"O, ye of little faith, why do you doubt?" How often Our Lord addressed this tender reproach to His beloved Twelve when they did not turn trustingly to Him in their personal needs; and He continues to speak those words to us today. It is as though God seeks to gauge our faith in Him in small ways. Can it be that we fail in prayer because of lack of faith? Are we afraid to ask a personal favor, as though God could not grant it? Why not be generous in casting out all doubt, and in taking with glad confidence the gifts of the Friend of our souls? Are we afraid that "having Him, we might have naught beside"?

Much of God's plan for the work He has given us to do may depend on our seeking from Him the results desired. At least we know this, that God's saints, His most familiar friends, were the boldest of all mortals in asking favors of Him. Don Bosco and the Cure of Ars, for example, seemed almost reckless in their confidence in God's bounty. After the death of Bishop James A. Walsh, the Co-Founder of Maryknoll, the late Archbishop McNicholas of Cincinnati said of his friend of many years: "His trust in Divine Providence seemed to me that of a saint. . . . He thought of his apostolate as God's work, and he took it as a simple matter of course that God would not fail on His part."

God's way with man is simple and homely. It is we who stand aloof and with stiff formality complicate relations instead of trusting swiftly and directly in His desire to help us. We dare to be hypocrites even with God. We aspire to elevated, majestic, resounding phrases in our intimate relations with Him, when what He wants most is that we trustingly tell Him in our own words what we need. We are like hypochondriacs who have memorized medical terminology and do not really seek efficient help from the doctor. We are so conscious of our "Sunday, go-to-meeting clothes" and our decorous posture that our prayers are apt to be sterile. Yet we are of the household of God. He is our Father and we should run to meet Him with all the prattle of our daily hurts and needs, confident that once we have told Him, He will take care of things.

The world and we are suffering from artificiality, from unreal aloofness from God, from a spirit of weak faith and too much self-reliance. To bring God into our lives, we must lean on Him. That means consciousness of our puny strength and of His power; it means trust in Him even for our daily needs, trust expressed in simple demands with confidence that He will grant them.

As we pray with the Church for the universal needs of mankind, let us also add our intimate requests for personal gifts, for specific favors for our work, for definite intentions of those in whom we are interested. And let us make these prayers of petition with the assurance that God is interested in whatever interests us, that He will make His own our cause and will reward our gesture of confidence by giving us what we ask Him for. Perhaps the conversion of our parish is waiting on such a request.

Come, Holy Spirit, kindle our cold hearts with Thy Fire of Love, so that purified of all the self seeking that separates us from the Blessed Trinity, we may grow in the depth and the breadth and the glory of our friendship with God.

# Eighteen

# Give Us Thy Sevenfold, Sacred Gifts

"Give to Thy faithful, who confide in Thee, Thy sevenfold, sacred gifts." This is a prayer that we should say often and fervently to God the Holy Spirit because, as St. Thomas Aquinas expressly tells us, the gifts of the Holy Spirit are necessary for the securing of salvation. I remember the first time I gave Confirmation to the Chinese Christians at Siaolok and how, filled with zeal, I launched into a sermon on the gifts of the Holy Spirit. After I had talked for about an hour and a half, I realized that perhaps I lacked wisdom; and they lacked understanding. But those Chinese converts certainly had the gift of fortitude!

Recalling the above experience, I shall not try to do more in these few pages than to speak of the gifts of the Holy Spirit in general. When in the Sacrament of Baptism we are born of water and the Holy Spirit, God gives us a share in the divine life of the Most Blessed Trinity. But we still have our weak bodies with all their imperfections and our vacillating wills that are so easily led astray. We have been elevated by grace; but our motives and acts still have a certain stamp of humanness about them that unfits us for the supernatural life. So the Holy Spirit bestows on us His sevenfold, sacred gifts, in order that we may become worthy children of Our Father in Heaven and thus attain to the happiness of dwelling with Him for all eternity.

When the Son of God became man, the Blessed Trinity prepared Him for His role on earth. In the inspired prophecy of Isaiah, we find the passage: "There shall come forth a rod out of the root of Jesse, and a flower shall rise up out of his root. And the spirit of the Lord shall rest upon Him: the spirit of wisdom and of understanding, the spirit of counsel and of fortitude, the spirit of knowledge and of godliness. And He shall be filled with the spirit of the fear of the Lord" *(Isai. XI: 1–3).*

By His Passion and death on the Cross, Christ, our Elder Brother, merited for us that we should become the adopted sons of God; and that we, too, should receive the gifts of the Holy Spirit. Christ bade His followers to be "perfect as your Heavenly Father is perfect" *(Matt. V: 48).* Our Lord could direct His disciples toward this supernatural goal, because He had gone before them in the way; and He had merited for them the means to achieve Beatitude, life as it is lived by God.

## Fear of the Lord and Godliness

The sevenfold, sacred gifts of the Holy Spirit do not replace the virtues of Faith, Hope, and Charity, which are fundamental to the divine life of a soul that has been baptized. Rather, they strengthen Faith in us; make our Hope more constant; and inflame our Charity. They direct us and guide us, fortify us and nourish us, for every duty we are called upon to perform on earth.

As we read in the Book of Psalms, "The fear of the Lord is the beginning of wisdom" *(Ps. CX: 10)*. It is not a slavish fear, but one that is founded on love. We fear to displease Our Father by our human frailty, and the Holy Spirit strengthens this salutary dread in us for our sanctification. There is nothing of cowardice in Christian fear of the Lord. It enables us to surmount a worldly desire of human esteem, and to withstand with equanimity unkind and unjust criticism. "Fear ye not them that kill the body and are not able to kill the soul: but rather fear him that can destroy both soul and body in hell" *(Matt. X: 28)*.

Godliness, or piety, is the instinctive turning of a child to its parents. It is a devotion compounded of reverence and love. Our Lord sent to us the Holy Spirit, the Spirit of Love, by Whom we call God, "Abba," Father. This Spirit of Love enables us to realize God's presence in a warm, trustful manner, as we give Him the worship of affectionate children. Piety also makes it possible for us to realize the presence of God in His earthly representatives:

our parents, religious superiors, and lawfully appointed secular rulers. Obedience is never servile, when piety makes us see duly constituted authority as coming from God, Our Father and Our Creator.

## Knowledge and Fortitude

Of ourselves, we cannot have a knowledge of God which will direct us unerringly to our heavenly goal, so we must ask the Holy Spirit to illumine our path. We see how far purely human knowledge falls short of apprehending the divine life in the case of certain learned men deeply versed in the natural sciences. When these distinguished scientists speak of the things of God, they often make stupid blunders that a Catholic child in the first communion class would avoid.

St. Thomas Aquinas explains by a very apt illustration why human reason alone does not suffice to guide us to eternal life with God. He says: "A medical student who has but an imperfect hold on the art of surgery cannot successfully carry through a delicate operation unless he is aided by his master." In like manner, without the aid of the Divine Surgeon, we lack sufficient knowledge to perform the crucial operation of cutting away from our souls the malignancies that unfit us for eternal union with the Blessed Trinity.

Together with prudence, justice, and temperance, fortitude is one of the cardinal virtues, one of the four chief natural virtues. The cardinal virtue of fortitude gives a man courage in the face of danger. The Fortitude that is a gift of the Holy Spirit supernaturalizes that courage by strong patience and endurance. It makes the Christian stand firm in the lifelong combat against the enemies of his soul.

The virtue of courage enables a soldier to advance in the face of deadly gunfire. But the Christian called upon to endure long imprisonment and protracted mental torture at the hands of the Communists cannot prevail without the fortitude that is the gift of God the Holy Spirit. It was not mere human fortitude that enabled Cardinal Mindszenty to face the expectation of being fiendishly deprived of his very reason, for Christ's sake.

## Understanding and Counsel

The Scriptures tell us that the Lord appeared to the young King Solomon in a dream by night, saying: "Ask what thou wilt that I should give thee."

Solomon answered: "Give to thy servant an understanding heart, to judge thy people, and discern between good and evil." God was pleased with the young ruler's request and gave him a wise and understanding heart, so that Solomon became a mightier king than his father, David *(III Kings III: 5–14).*

The French have a saying: "To understand all is to pardon all." We cannot have in our souls the compassionate charity of Christ unless the Holy Spirit gives us an understanding heart. Let us pray to Him, then, to grant us the ability to distinguish between what is important and what is of no consequence. St. Paul tells us that "the Spirit searches all things, yea, the deep things of God" *(I Cor. II: 10).* Out of the infinite depth of His own Understanding, the Third Person of the Blessed Trinity can bring us to realize the importance of eternal values.

The gift of counsel teaches us to listen to the voice of God when we pray. He is always calling us to greater perfection, to greater proofs of our love for Him; but we are often so preoccupied with talking about our real or imaginary needs that we do not heed the Divine inspirations. The gift of counsel will also incline us to seek readily the advice of God's representatives on earth.

God is speaking to some of us in the same manner that He spoke to the rich young man in the Gospels, who came seeking to be a disciple of Christ. This young ruler had kept all the commandments from his youth and when Jesus looked on him, He loved him. So our Lord gave this seeker after everlasting life a counsel of perfection. If we ask God the Holy Spirit to strengthen and enlighten our souls with His gift of counsel, we shall not become sorrowful, like the rich young man, when

Christ invites us to surrender prized possessions the better to follow Him.

## The Crowning Gift

The crowning gift of the Holy Spirit is the gift of wisdom, because it regulates and coordinates all the other gifts. Naturally speaking, there is an infinite distance between the reason of man and the wisdom of God. "For the wisdom of the flesh is death: but the wisdom of the spirit is life and peace" *(Rom.VIII: 6)*.

When the Blessed Virgin was an obscure maiden in the village of Nazareth, the Holy Spirit flooded her pure soul with wisdom, so that she consented to cooperate in the salvation of mankind by becoming the Mother of God. During every instant of his earthly life, Our Lord was full of the wisdom of the Holy Spirit. Indeed, we are expressly told that the Child Jesus "grew in this wisdom."

Christ merited for us that the same Spirit which informed all His Divine thoughts and actions while He was in the flesh should dwell also in our imperfect souls. God the Holy Spirit initiated our souls into the divine life of God by grace; let us beg Him to keep them on the way to heaven by a constant infusion of His sevenfold, sacred gifts. "Thy good Spirit shall lead me into the land where is my destiny" *(Ps. CXLII: 10)*.

In this land of beatitude, the glorified soul will embrace God, through God; that is to say, through the Holy Spirit. "We see now through a glass in a dark manner; but then face to face. Now I know in part: but then I shall know even as I am known" *(1 Cor. XIII: 12).*

## Nineteen

# Grant Us Salvation in the End

In our study of the Sequence for Pentecost, we have been examining the action of God the Holy Spirit on our souls. There is nothing new in this doctrine. The Third Person of the Blessed Trinity has been with the world from the very beginning, and He has been with each one of us in a special manner since our baptism. He has made our hearts temples dedicated to His service, temples in which He expects us to keep His light shining perpetually before men, so that they may glorify their Father Who is in heaven.

### Sanctity of the Christian Soul

From our childhood, we Catholics have been told of the indwelling of God the Holy Spirit in our souls; but has this stupendous truth ever really come home to us? We read in the First Epistle of St. Paul to the Corinthians:

"Know you not that you are the temple of God and that the Spirit of God dwelleth in you? But if any man violate the temple of God, him shall God destroy. For the temple of God is holy, which you are" *(I Cor. III: 16, 17)*.

If we acquire the habit of thinking with awe and boundless thanksgiving that our own souls are shrines of the Holy Spirit, the possibility of desecrating such a holy place will seem to us more terrible by far than the death of the body. Is it not because the Communists have rejected as superstition any belief in the indwelling of God in the soul that they have lost all respect for the human individual? We have an urgent duty to pray and to make reparation for those who violate the temple of God in their own souls and seek to drive out the Holy Spirit from the souls of the young.

The whole study of the action of God the Holy Spirit on our souls should show us how much we need His grace, His light, and His strength. The work that as Christians we are trying to accomplish is not *our* work, but His. Our Lord told us, "I am the Vine and you are the branches." Separated from the Vine, the branches do not bear fruit; they gradually wither away *(John XV: 5)*.

The trials and the misunderstandings we encounter in life do not become an unbearable burden when we recall that they are the responsibility of the Holy Spirit, because we are doing His work. We have an All-Powerful Partner in our work for God; even though we ourselves are only unprofitable servants.

So we come to the final appeals to the Holy Spirit in the Sequence for Pentecost. Knowing that He loves us with an everlasting tenderness, we say to Him with perfect confidence in His generosity: "Give us the grace we need; give us especially the grace of final perseverance; grant us salvation in the end."

## Mother of Beautiful Love

Whenever I speak or write for any length of time about the things of God, I always seem to see somewhere close to me Father Price, the holy spiritual director of the pioneer Maryknoll students and the first Maryknoller to die in China. I hear him asking us students, so long ago, "What shall we talk about?" With one voice we would answer what we knew would please him, "Talk to us about the Blessed Virgin." "All right," he would say, "we will talk about the Immaculate Conception." So, here and now, I am still following Father Price's lead.

Indeed, it would seem strange if we should speak of the Holy Spirit without singing the praises of His Virgin Spouse, of her who by the power of the Holy Spirit became the Mother of God. The Holy Spirit came to dwell in our souls at baptism; but from the first moment of Our Lady's conception, the Spirit of God took possession of her soul. "I to my beloved, and my beloved to me, who feedeth among the lilies" *(Cant. II: 16)*.

All during her earthly life, the Blessed Virgin never ceased to advance in grace because, unlike us, she always was gladly obedient to the whisperings of the Holy Spirit. Thus, she produced in their full splendor the fruits of God the Holy Spirit. In the Gospel for the Vigil of the Feast of the Immaculate Conception of the Blessed Virgin Mary, we read: "My fruits are those of sincerity and honor, and I am the Mother of Beautiful Love. I am the Mother of Understanding; I am the Mother of Holy Hope."

She who is "our tainted nature's solitary boast" has said to us: "Learn of me; follow my ways." We have in Mary of Nazareth a perfect model of the effulgent sanctity resulting from the undeviating correspondence of a soul with the promptings of the Holy Spirit. Grant us, O Lord, that even as we proclaim Thy spotless Mother to have been preserved by Thy grace from all stain, so may we be delivered, by her intercession, from all our sins.

The Holy Spirit overshadows our own baptized souls and calls upon us to cooperate in the work of the redemption of mankind. The glory of God waits upon our poor human consent. Let us pray to Mary, our model, that our answer may be the same as hers: "Be it done unto me according to Thy word. Thy kingdom come; Thy will be done."

Then we, too, can exult, "My soul doth magnify the Lord." We, too, can say with Our Lady, "Behold the servant of the Lord." This title of servant of God will be our proudest possession on earth, and our password to heaven.

The language of the Church is true; it means what it says. God the Holy Spirit, the Spirit of Love of the Holy Trinity, has in all truth overshadowed us and claimed us body and soul as His possession. He has infused into our souls the gifts of wisdom, counsel, understanding, fortitude, knowledge, piety, and fear of the Lord. He is willing and anxious to set our hearts on fire and to send us out into our life's work confident in Him.

## Servant of God Francis X. Ford

*Bishop and Martyr (1892–1952)*

In 1912, Francis Ford, straight out of high school in Brooklyn, became the first recruit to join the new Maryknoll Fathers and Brothers, a missionary society founded the previous year. In 1918, following his ordination, he joined the first group of four Maryknoll priests to embark on a mission to China.

In Kaying, in southern China, where he spent more than twenty years, he saw the Catholic population increase to twenty thousand. Eventually he would be appointed as its first bishop. He loved his flock and reminded fellow clergy to encounter the Chinese in a spirit of "reverence, respect, and love, a meeting of brothers." He especially welcomed the Maryknoll Sisters, recognizing their facility in entering the world of Chinese women. "Hours spent in the chapel are not the only means of entertaining the Beloved Guest of the soul. We can often please Him better when we are out in the highways and byways of China, offering to needy souls the hospitality of our Christian love."

Ford remained in China throughout the war. But in 1950, following the Communist Revolution, he was placed under house arrest and charged with espionage. Though never tried, he was starved, beaten, and regularly paraded before mocking crowds. He died in prison on February 21, 1952. His cause for canonization is in process.

> *Grant us . . . to be the doorstep by which the multitudes may come to Thee. And if . . . we are ground underfoot and spat upon and worn out, at least we . . . shall become the King's Highway in pathless China.*
>
> —Bishop Francis X. Ford